ENTREPRENEURSHIP: THE BOTTOM LINE

HOW 17 HIGH SCHOOL SENIORS WROTE A BUSINESS PLAN, RAISED CAPITAL, STARTED AND OPERATED A BUSINESS WITHIN 127 DAYS

A TRUE STORY

Lake Highland Entrepreneurs, LLC.
Copyrighted 2008

iUniverse, Inc.
New York   Bloomington

Entrepreneurship: The Bottom Line

iUniverse books may be ordered through booksellers or by contacting:

iUniverse
1663 Liberty Drive
Bloomington, IN 47403
www.iuniverse.com
1-800-Authors (1-800-288-4677)

ISBN: 978-1-4401-2898-1 (pbk)
ISBN: 978-1-4401-2897-4 (ebk)

Printed in the United States of America

iUniverse rev. date: 6/8/2009

Preface

It's been reported that up to 98% of all businesses in America fail. In fact, in a well-circulated Youtube video, "Shift Happens", it is reported that China and India have more honor students than we have students. In short, the video explained how the Global Economy is shifting the power away from the U.S. How can this problem be solved when the U.S. government spends less than 70 million dollars a year (less than half of what Nintendo spends annually on marketing) on a failing public education system? How can students, parents, and/or aspiring entrepreneurs obtain the tools necessary to conquer this problem?

The answer lies within our school systems' ability to innovate.

Lake Highland Preparatory School is accepting this challenge.

In January, seventeen high school students formed a limited liability company to produce the ultimate entrepreneurial handbook- Entrepreneurship: The Bottom Line. This manual/ journal captures the real world challenges of entrepreneurialism in a clear, concise and compelling story, presenting how most of these challenges can be overcome. This is a prime example of what entrepreneurialism is all about.

TABLE OF CONTENTS   PAGE

THE IDEA:
BOB VANDER LUGT AND MARK HAYES   6

INTRODUCTION:
CONCEPTS OF ENTREPRENEURIALISM   10

I.   BEING A LEADER: 14
        Entrepreneurialism is a challenge that anyone can
        partake in, but few can master.

        a.   WILL MADDUX - CEO
        b.   EMPLOYEES
                i.   LEADERSHIP
                ii.   TRUST
                iii.   ATTITUDE

II.   BUSINESS PLAN: 24
        A house is never built without a blueprint and a
        business is never started without a business plan.

        a.   ADAM MAALI - COO
                i.   WHAT IS A COO?
                ii.   BUSINESS PLAN

III.   FINANCE: 36
        Business, just like the rest of the world, revolves
        around money, so always count your pennies.

        a.   KAYLEN JAMES – CFO
        b.   PRASHANT RAJU – DIR. OF FINANCE

i.   ACCOUNTING
ii.   BANKING
iii.   INVESTMENT
iv.   PRICE OF YOUR COMPANY
v.   BUDGETING
vi.   PROFIT AND LOSS STATEMENTS
vii.   DEBT EQUITY

IV.   MARKETING: 56

Marketing requires confidence and innovation. It takes a feeling or even a gutsy impulse of just putting your ideas out on the line hoping for success. Constant improvement is an utter necessity as new ideas are always flowing, each new idea seeming better and more exciting than the last. The customer isn't always going to come to you; you need to figure out how you can reach them and reaching them is imperative to effectively marketing what you are trying to sell.

a.   MAGGIE MARTINEZ – CMO
b.   TAYLOR OWEN – DIR. OF MARKETING
     i.   THREE POINTS TO MARKETING
c.   ZACH HAAS – CIO
     i.   THREE POINTS TO INNOVATION
     ii.   INNOVATION
     iii.   TARGET MARKET
     iv.   DEMOGRAPHICS
     v.   GEOGRAPHIC AND LIFESTYLE FACTORS
     vi.   CUSTOMER NEEDS
     vii. ADVERTISING
     viii. PROMOTIONS
     ix.   MARKETING NICHE
     x.   MARKETING ENVIRONMENT

xi.   BUSINESS STYLE AND
ETIQUETTE

V.   ART: 78

The Art Director is responsible for giving a fresh innovative look to your product, service or company. They must assess the interests of the consumer and work with the marketing department to creating something that is aesthetically appealing.

a.   TAYLOR GRENNIP – ART DIRECTOR
       i.   UNIQUENESS
       ii.   CLARITY
       iii.   COLOR
       iv.   GRAPHIC DESIGN
       v.   CREATIVITY

VI.   PUBLIC RELATIONS: 82

Public relations is all about first getting a handle on what your product is so that you can successfully advertise it to the public working with those around you to present your product/service in the best possible light. It then involves finding different outlets to expose your idea to the market it was meant to reach.

a.   JOSH KORSHACK – DIRECTOR OF
PUBLIC RELATIONS
b.   JAYMEE LEFFLER - DIRECTOR OF
PUBLIC RELATIONS
c.   CAMERON TALLON - DIRECTOR OF
PUBLIC RELATIONS
       i.   THREE POINTS TO
PUBLIC RELATIONS
       ii.   WRITING A PRESS RELEASE

VII.   SALES: **90**
Sales involves selling your product by gaining support from others so that you can successfully achieve what you have set out to and then assessing your competition and determining price by looking at competitors to make   your own product/service stand out.

    a.   **MARK JENSEN – DIRECTOR OF SALES**
    b.   **CAMERON TALLON – ACCT. EXEC.**
    c.   **GRAHAM GRINDSTAFF – ACCT EXEC.**
        i.   **SALESMANSHIP**
        ii.   **SALES PLAN**
        iii.   **PRESENTATION**
        iv.   **NEGOTIATION**

VIII.   DISTRIBUTION: **112**
Distribution consists of the storing, packaging, and actual shipping of the product as well as figuring out the price so that the business can profit from it.

    a.   **NICK KEENER – DIR. OF DISTRIBUTION**
        i.   **THREE POINTS TO DISTRIBUTION**
        ii.   **SHIPPING**
        iii.   **STORAGE**
        iv.   **PROFIT**
        v.   **DISTRIBUTION DIRECTOR**

IX.   ADMINISTRATION & HUMAN RESOURCES: **116**
    a.   **ALEXIS CHARRAN – CAO**
        i.   **ADMINISTRATION**
        ii.   **WAGES**
        iii.   **POLICIES**
        iv.   **BENEFITS**
        v.   **BOARD MEETINGS**

X.   EXIT STRATEGY: **124**
Determining the value of your product/service is
imperative to the future of your company telling
you whether it is a smart idea to continue progress
or sell it when it is at its peak of profit to you, the
creator. It is all about weighing your losses and
seeing into the future... however impossible that
may seem.

> a.   **BLAKE MAHER – DIRECTOR OF**
>   **MERGERS AND ACQUISITIONS**
>   i.   **VALUATION**
>   ii.   **SELLING YOUR BUSINESS**

XI.   LAKE HIGHLAND ENTREPRENEURS: **130**
>   a.   **WHAT WE'VE LEARNED**

XII. SPONSORS   **131**

XIII. APPENDIX: **132**

>   a.   **REFERENCES**

Bob Vander Lugt, J.D.
Lake Highland Preparatory School Faculty

In the 2007 school year I was asked to assist in teaching a new course called "Entrepreneurship" during the following year. I worked with a Lake Highland (LHP) Board Member to structure a course without a textbook. Our concept was to teach a "hands-on", very practical course based on the decades of his experience in business and mine in law and teaching.

As the school year approached, my business mentor moved from Orlando; the LHP administration nevertheless determined to press on with our plan. Another local entrepreneur, Mark Hayes, agreed to share his years of entrepreneurship experience and he began to outline the content of a course that would   provide the "real world" approach desired.

Textbooks addressing entrepreneurship for high school

students are available. But the approach of this course has excited and energized our students largely because they had no book to follow. They simply had to forge their way through the challenges and learn by their mistakes and successes.

Our 17 students were not selected by anyone for this class. They individually chose to enter a course about which they knew very little; there were no prior students to counsel them. We have seen that high school students can, with knowledgeable guidance and encouragement, do everything required to succeed in an entrepreneurship venture. It has become a rewarding learning adventure—with Adam Smith's "invisible hand" of profit a part of the lure. This book, as their product, is the compelling evidence that our teens do embrace free market opportunities if offered to them.

Lake Highland will continue to offer this course to give students a unique learning experience. We encourage other schools to share our vision of teaching our teens how to keep America's economic dreams alive and thriving.

Administrative Quotes:

"Great institutional thanks to you and Mark for the inspirational leadership you give these students. The progress of the last few months reflects the struggles and triumphs any good educational experience should have. The students' presentations were impressive for so many reasons: their poise, level of preparation, articulation and enthusiasm. Their discoveries will help them be successful in all future endeavors. I am proud to be a High-lander." - Susan Clayton | **Vice President for Advancement**

"I commend you for your openness, flexibility and trust in the process at the start of this two years ago, through all its vicissitudes. We didn't know exactly where we were going with this and it broke new ground. ...Allowing others to lead has produced a wonderful learning experience for our seniors. Congratulations and thank you for the hard work. We'll see ho wit unfolds...we're not done yet!" - Kathy Taylor | **Special Assistant to the President for Curriculum and Academics**

Mark Hayes, CCIM
CEO - Atlantic Management, Inc.

For over seven years I had the pleasure of working with young students throughout Orange County, Florida through a volunteer program provided by Junior Achievement. I have always been passionate about education but never so much as when my wife informed me that we were having a baby. I had met with several administrators from Lake Highland about a class on entrepreneurism and was very excited when they invited me to help them create a new curriculum on business and entrepreneurism. However, the idea of just teaching a class on entrepreneurism just didn't feel right with me given the caliber of talent at Lake Highland.

I had volunteered multiple times at Lake Highland and felt that if ever there was a campus to produce the next Bill Gates, Lake Highland was it.   On the morning that my daughter was born, November 6, 2007 (I couldn't sleep), I decided that if I was going to really prepare these young students for the real world then they needed to start a real company and face the real challenges of entrepreneurism.

I was convinced that if any school could pull this off, it was Lake Highland. The student's talent and passion for running a business far exceeded my expectations.   I am now even more convinced that a Lake Highland student will very soon run a company that will change our world.

I want to thank everyone at Lake Highland for committing to this experiment and also thank the vendors, speakers and investors who contributed to the success of this project. We hope this book inspires other young entrepreneurs to follow their dreams.

INTRODUCTION

Summary: 127 Days in a Nutshell

Idea of Entrepreneurialism:

Entrepreneur- (n.) a person who organizes and operates a business or businesses, taking on greater than normal financial risks in order to do so.

AND RISKS ARE EXACTLY WHAT WE TOOK...

Seventeen Lake Highland Seniors joined the class "Entrepreneurship" for different reasons. Some were looking to learn the basics of business in order to be prepared for one day starting their own, where others were simply intrigued by young enterprising entrepreneurs and looked to learn more about the phenomenon that is ENTREPRENEURSHIP. Showing up for class on the first day, the students were greeted not with shiny new textbooks titled Entrepreneurship 101... but a successful businessman ready to take the class down the road... never traveled.

We had:

- **NO TIME** (127 days to be exact)
- **NO MONEY** (quickly racking up fees)
- **NO CLUE ABOUT BUSINESS**

And with this... we set off on the same journey many of you are about to take, and learned our way through starting our own business.

An entrepreneur is a person who organizes, operates, and assumes the risk for a business venture. They organize who does what and how they will be selling the product, operating the process

10

of advertising, constructing the product, and generally running the company itself. Assuming great risk is what separates great entrepreneurs from the unmotivated, cautious Average Joe holding a great idea. Many of these great entrepreneurs put their own money, home, and most of all, their reputation on the line. Not all people are cut out to live the dangerous life of an entrepreneur. The future is unsure and the weight of this can be extremely stressful, however, in the end all the headache and struggle you have endured makes success all that much more rewarding.

Being an entrepreneur is what encompasses the American dream. It's taking an idea of your own and working your butt off to reach set goals. Far too often these days people fail. This may be due to lack of motivation or flat out fiscal mismanagement. However, with the right tools and guidance, your entrepreneurial dream can become a reality.

Entrepreneurship is a great magnet for new ideas, unique approaches, and innovative technologies. When conducted in the proper way, turning people into entrepreneurs improves a country's economic situation and aids sustainable progress. However, transition to become an entrepreneur is not equally attractive to all. Risks and uncertainties involved in starting a new business coupled with a stagnant economy discourage people from stepping up the plate and taking a swing.

Concepts of Entrepreneurialism:

Entrepreneurialism can be defined in many different ways and entrepreneurs come in many shapes and forms. It entails a person who creates, runs, and takes on the risk and reward of business. Entrepreneurialism and its concepts deal with leadership, control, and risk. Every entrepreneur is a leader because they don't let others set their tariff. They create and lead the way in every business venture. An entrepreneur must ensure that the "business" will be financially successful; therefore, they must control or guide the company as a whole to make sure that success is reached. Risk is not just a board game; it is what entrepreneurs thrive on. Risk is a two-fold advantage in entrepreneurialism. Any good entrepreneur loves the reward that risk brings and takes advantage of others shying away from it. Overall, the concepts of entrepreneurialism could make a list longer than this book, but the above mentioned can fit into the ideas of leadership, control, and risk.

Lake Highland | **Entrepreneurs, LLC**

I. BEING A LEADER

Will Maddux
Chief Executive Officer

* *"If you want to be the CEO you have to keep in mind the buck stops with you. The end."*
* *"Starting a business is actually rather easy. Keeping it going is what is difficult."*
* *"I'll give you the definition of my job. Responsibility. I won't say it's good or bad, but it's different from any job I've had before."*

Employees

"Being the CEO of a company is a lot of hard work that requires organization and leadership, but the experience is priceless."

- Leadership
- Trust
- Attitude

Leadership:

Leadership is the cornerstone quality of any businessman or woman that holds a position of influence. Without leadership not one fortune five hundred company would be where it is today, in fact, not even one company can be successful without leadership.

Leadership is the process of directing the behavior of others toward the accomplishment of some common objective.

"Leadership is influencing people to get things done to a standard and quality above their norm...and doing it willingly."

As an element in social interaction, leadership is a complex activity involving:

- A process of influence
- Actors who are both leaders and followers
- A range of possible outcomes - the achievement of goals, but also the commitment of individuals to such goals as well as the enhancement of group cohesion.

Building Better Leaders through Attributes:

Leadership attributes are the inner or personal qualities that constitute effective leadership. These attributes include a large array of characteristics such as values, character, motives, habits, traits, style, behaviors, and skills.

The Foundation of Leadership: Achieving Extraordinary Results By Brian Tracy

"The most important quality of leadership, the one quality for which you want to be known, is extraordinary performance, with the goal of achieving extraordinary results. These results then serve as an inspiration to others to perform at equally exceptional levels. People ascribe leadership to those men and women whom they feel can most enable them to achieve important goals or objectives."

Learning to Lead:
Effective leaders recognize that what they know is very little in comparison to what they still need to learn. To be more proficient in pursuing and achieving objectives, you should be open to new ideas, insights, and revelations that can lead to better ways of accomplishing goals. This continuous learning process can be exercised, in particular, through engaging yourself in a constant dialogue with your peers, advisers, consultants, team members, suppliers, customers, and competitors.

Leading others is not simply a matter of style, or following some how-to guides or recipes. Ineffectiveness of leaders seldom results from a lack of know-how or how-to, nor is it typically due to inadequate managerial skills. Leadership is not even about creating a great vision. It is about creating conditions under which all your followers can perform independently and effectively toward a common objective.

James O' Tool, a noted management theorist, proposes a new vision of leadership in the business world - a values-based leadership that is not only fair and just, but also highly effective in today's complex organizations. It is based on:

* your ideas and values

- your understanding of the differing and conflicting needs of your followers
- your ability to energize followers to pursue a better goal than they had thought possible
- your skills in creating a values-based umbrella large enough to accommodate the various interests of followers, but focused enough to direct all their energies in pursuit of a common goal

Trust:

Trust is both an emotional and logical act. Emotionally, it is where you expose your vulnerabilities to people while believing they will not take advantage of your openness. Logically, it is where you have assessed the probabilities of gain and loss, calculating expected utility based on hard performance data, and concluded that the person in question will behave in a predictable manner. In practice, trust is a bit of both. I trust you because I have experienced your trustworthiness and because I have faith in human nature.

We feel trust. Emotions associated with trust include companionship, friendship, love, agreement, relaxation, comfort. There are a number of different ways we can define trust. Here are the dimensions of trust and consequent definitions.

Predictability:

It is a normal part of the human condition to be constantly forecasting ahead. We build internal models of the world based both on our experiences and what others tell us, and then use these to guess what will happen next. This allows us to spot and prepare for threats and also make plans to achieve our longer-term goals.

The greatest unpredictability is at 50%; a reliable enemy can be preferable to an unpredictable friend, as at least we know where we stand with them.

DEFINITION 1: Trust means being able to predict what other people will do and what situations will occur. If we can surround ourselves with people we trust, then we can create a safe present and an even better future.

Value exchange:

Most of what we do with other people is based around exchange, which is the basis for all businesses as well as simple relationships. At its simplest, it is an exchange of goods. I will swap you two sheep for one cow. It is easy to calculate the value in such material bargaining. Things get more complex when less tangible forces come into play. A parent exchanges attention for love. A company exchanges not only pay but good working conditions for the intellectual and manual efforts of its workforce.

Value exchange works because we each value things differently. If I have a whole flock of sheep but no milk, then I can do business with a person who has a herd of cows but no clothes. This principle of reciprocity is what binds societies together.

Trust in value exchange occurs when we do not know fully whether what we are receiving is what we expect. When we buy a car, don't want to be sold a ringer which the seller knows is faulty. When I get advice in business, I want it to be based on facts, not wild opinions.

DEFINITION 2: Trust means making an exchange with someone when you do not have full knowledge about them, their intent and the things they are offering to you.

Delayed Reciprocity:

Exchange is not just about an immediate swapping of cows and sheep or hugs and kisses. What makes companies and societies really work is that something is given now, but the return is paid back some time in the future. The advantage of this is that we can create a more flexible environment, where you can get what you need when you need it, rather than having to save up for it.

Trust now becomes particularly important, because otherwise we are giving something for nothing. The delay we have placed in the reciprocal arrangement adds a high level of uncertainty which we need to mitigate through trust.

What is often called the 'golden rule' is a simple formula for creating trust. 'Do unto others as you would have them do unto you.' It sets up the dynamic for my giving you something now with the hope of getting back some unspecified thing in the indeterminate future.

DEFINITION 3: Trust means giving something now withan expectation that it will be repaid, possibly in some unspecified way at some unspecified time in the future.

Exposed Vulnerabilities:

When we trust other people, we may not only be giving them something in hope of getting something else back in the future, we may also be exposing ourselves in a way that others can take advantage of our vulnerabilities. If I buy a car from you and I do not know a good price, you can lie to me so you get a better bargain. If I tell you in confidence about the problems I am having with work, you could use this to further your own career at my expense.

Although the threat of retribution or projected feelings of guilt can counteract your temptation to abuse my exposed vulnerabilities, if you succumb I still get hurt and may still end up with the shorter stick. For our transaction to complete successfully, I must be able to trust that such agonies will not come to pass.

Attitude:

Written for SA Career Focus by Wayne Mallinson

"Here's a secret: your attitude is probably going to be one of the biggest determining factors for your future success in your career. Sure, skills, work support, and values will also play a part, but attitude is what you will be known (and remembered) by. Attitude will determine your altitude in your career.

Some companies spell it out in their marketing brochures: We hire for attitude and train for skill. To be frighteningly honest, you need to pay attention to your attitude as you are growing up. A smart company will uncover your existing attitude in or even before the job interview. Not only must you must pay attention to attitude during a job interview, but also when you have landed the job. Attitude is very easy for your managers and colleagues to measure, and measure they will, even if you and they do not realize it, people are always summing each other up.

Attitudes express themselves through words and actions, for example, "always works hard", shows in people who are willing to take on extra tasks or responsibilities, the words are, "I'll do it." "Constantly grumbles", is easy to discover. "Is trustworthy", is not likely to be the office gossip.

We will all immediately recognize a bad attitude by what people say. It's not my job. It's not my problem. 'What's in it for me? Do I have to do this? Here are some examples of employee-attitudes that might not go down well when there is work to be done. It is sometimes difficult to make a judgment call, because in some cases a lazy manager will download his or her tasks onto you unfairly. However, don't despair. Lazy managers would already have been identified by their superiors for their lazy attitude!

It's even easier (certainly more refreshing) to spot a good attitude. Attitude says something about who a person is, rather than what they do or know. Therefore, someone who says, "Thank you" when helped, is grateful. Someone who says, "Please, could you help me here?" is willing to learn and keen to keep the job moving. Someone who says, "It was really John's good idea", is being trustworthy to a colleague rather than being self-seeking.

It is always much more pleasant to be around persons with a positive outlook on life, than their cranky opposites. Positive people will generally attract more help from colleagues, more satisfaction from customers, and more sales than the average person will. Negative people do have some valuable contributions and add a perspective to what might go wrong, but other than that, are often less productive and less well- connected to fellow workers and customers.

There is an often-quoted story that states: An optimist is someone who sees a glass as half-full, whereas a pessimist sees the same glass as half-empty. But I'll have none of this. Both of those attitudes are neutral to me. A real pessimist is someone who can see the half-empty glass and just know in their hearts that it will soon be knocked over and broken, and that they will be cut! A real optimist would have been less internally focused and seen the person coming around to offer a re-fill and then discuss a raise or a promotion!

I know who I would rather work with, I know who I would rather employ, I know who I would rather promote if I had the long-term good of my company at heart. Can attitude be changed? Yes, and right now! Think of one person who has helped you recently. Now lift the phone and thank them. Can't think of anyone? That's OK. Then get up right now and go and help someone, even if it's to get him or her some tea. Attitude is contagious. Start each day by consciously having a good attitude and it will go better for you and all around you. Attitude is an outward expression of who you are. Start practicing early, so that you can make the best of life.

Attitude can be expressed and measured in thousands of ways (words and actions). You may ask, is there one simple rule for knowing how to behave in a work situation? Yes there is! I have found a quick way to check my own attitude. I ask myself when on the job, How will the company or person who is paying for the work, best benefit from my actions? I then carry out that answer knowing that it is the right (although not always the easiest) thing to do."

THE BOTTOM LINE

Entrepreneurialism is a challenge that anyone can partake in, but few can master.

Quote From Professional:

"You are only as good as your last project"- **Will Maddux** - Hotel Development/Owner/Manager

Lake Highland | **Entrepreneurs, LLC**

Adam Maali
Chief Operating Officer

* *"This company made me realize how much work is involved and how very challenging, but fun and, hopefully rewarding, entrepreneurialism is."*
* *"The business plan is never final, and will always be changing."*
* *"Being a COO disciplined me in making deadlines, taking orders, and making them happen."*

COO:

A Chief Operating Officer or Chief Operations Officer (COO) is a corporate officer responsible for managing the day-to-day activities of the corporation. The COO is one of the highest ranking members of an organization, monitoring the daily operations of the company and reporting to the CEO and/or Board of Directors. The COO is usually an executive or senior vice president.

The chief operating officer is responsible for operations management (OM). The focus of the COO is on strategic, tactical, and short-term OM, which means he or she is responsible for the development, design, operation, and improvement of the systems that create and deliver the firm's products/services. Managers need to understand the real work behind the company's core operations, and the buck stops with the COO, whose primary concern is operations improvement. The duties of the COO may reside in certain organizations with a Vice President of Operations.

Current and aspiring Chief Operating Officers can achieve professional credentialing through the Certified Business Manager (CBM) program established by the Association of Professionals in Business Management.

Business Plan:

The business plan is one of the most important documents for the business. For investors, it is the most important thing to look at before investing in your company. The business plan is a detailed document discussing the financial, sales, marketing, and other important components of the company. The business plan can be extremely difficult to write, but with the right tools, it can become very easy. Also, be prepared to spend several weeks to finish the plan. When I was writing the business plan, I had no experience what so ever. I sat and stared at the computer for hours. However, I found several books and programs, which specialize in helping you write a business plan. I used one of these programs, and with step-by-step help, I finished the plan with ease, and within a couple of days.

Lake Highland Entrepreneurs (LHE) is raising $6,000 through debt instruments to cover half of the basic cost of goods and approximately 62% of the start up expenses. Each investor will receive a thirty percent (30%) return on their investment.

The projected sales over the duration of the first sales cycle should exceed $18,000 with the net margin projected to be 21%, producing net revenues exceeding $3,000.

The exit strategy for investors involves a corporate sale. Competitive analysis has shown that publishing companies are selling using a price earnings ratio (Revenue Factor) exceeding ten (10). LHE has conservatively projected

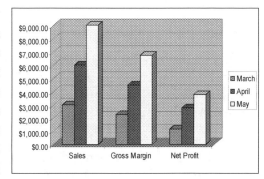

a price earnings ratio of three (3), producing a net sale exceeding $9,000, providing a 50% cushion ($6,000 / $12,000) for investor ROI.

1.1 Objectives

1. Sales of over $15 thousand by May of 2008
2. Gross margin higher than 70%
3. Net income more than 28% of sales by the third month

1.2 Mission

Lake Highland Entrepreneurs, LLC (LHE) will offer the knowledge on entrepreneurship at a price which is competitive in comparison to other business books in the market. We value our relationships with current and future customers and will communicate our appreciation to them through our outstanding product quality, personal service, and efficient delivery. Our commitment to our customers and the company will be reflected through honest and responsible business.

1.3 Keys to Success

To succeed LHE must:

* Implement a successful advertisement and marketing campaign to inform the public of our new company.
* Develop a niche market for our unique book.
* Maximize profits by selling through the Internet at full retail price.
* Develop a network with other businesses and experts, through interviews published on our website.

2.1 Company Summary

Lake Highland Entrepreneurs, LLC will be formed as a retail company specializing in marketing of its entrepreneurial book in household markets. Its founders are high school seniors, most of whom are starting their first company. They are founding Lake Highland Entrepreneurs, LLC to formalize the book they offer.

Lake Highland Entrepreneurs, LLC has an opportunity to be one of the first companies to be run by high school students. LHE is strong in drive and ability, yet it must stay focused to achieve its goal. Time must be handled carefully if it is to be a success.

2.2 Company Ownership

The company will be a closely-held Limited Liability Company with eighteen units who will form the Board of Directors. LHE has 1 million available shares and has only issued 500 thousand shares. Seventeen members will hold 14,411 shares each in the company, along with Mark Hayes being the majority member with 255,002 shares. It is owned and operated by these seventeen members.

Start-up Requirements	
Start-up Expenses	
Legal	$500
Website	$319
Yearbook	$150
Book Printing	$4,200
Other	$300
Total Start-up Expenses	$5,300
Start-up Assets	
Cash Required	$700
Other Current Assets	$0
Long-term Assets	$0
Total Assets	$700
Total Requirements	$6,000

Start-Up

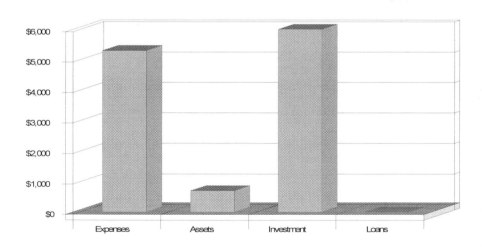

2.3 Start-Up Summary

Our start-up cost is $6,000. The money has primarily been used for legal fees, purchasing ads, and establishing a website. Upon receiving investments for the first month, we plan on heavy advertising through the Internet, business publications, newspapers, and various bookstores. The start-up costs are shown in the following table and illustration.

3. Products

The flagship product of Lake Highland Entrepreneurs, LLC is an Entrepreneurship book that can be used as a tool to learn about and teach entrepreneurialism. The book will be written by a ghost writer, and edited to our liking.

4. Market Analysis Summary

Lake Highland Entrepreneurs, LLC has many competitors as there are countless, how-to, books in the market. However, LHE sets itself above the rest, due to the fact that its competition lacks the personality of a young enterprising entrepreneur and the point of view of first-time entrepreneurs. With the hiring of Consensus Communications Inc, a public relations firm, LHE will advertise in business magazines, local newspapers, bookstores, and much more.

1.1 Market Segmentation

Lake Highland Entrepreneurs' advertisements are focused to over a hundred thousand customers. These customers include new entrepreneurs who are looking for guidance on starting a new business, parents who are looking to teach their children about business, and students who are looking to learn about business.

		March	April	May	
Potential Customers	Growth				CAGR
New Entrepreneurs	25%	384	480	600	25.02%
Parents	25%	128	160	200	25.05%
Students	25%	128	160	200	25.05%
Total	25.03%	640	800	1,000	25.03%

4.2 Target Market Segment Strategy

Lake Highland Entrepreneurs, LLC is directed towards young enterprising individuals looking to learn the basics they need to start a business, or grasp the spirit of entrepreneurialism. Our product is also geared towards parents, who wish to give their children the tools they need to succeed in the world of business, and are interested in giving them a head start on how to best channel the education they are receiving into future success.

5. Web Plan Summary

Lake Highland Entrepreneurs, LLC will be a dynamic marketing tool for the company that serves the needs of business development and sales. The company site will provide information about LHE's product for target customers and potential investors. As the company grows, its recruiting needs can be addressed by posting FAQs about the company, such as being the only company started by seventeen high school students according to some sources.

www.LakeHighlandEntrepreneurs.com will also communicate company news to create and maintain positive public relations with the community and investors. LHE will implement a functional and professionally designed website that can be adapted to meet the company's growing needs.

5.1 Development Requirements

Creation of future versions of the Lake Highland Entrepreneurs, LLC website will continue to be outsourced by a professional graphics designer. The contractor will work with the marketing department to conceptualize the company's logo and overall design. It will be maintained in-house.

6. Sales Strategy

There are other sources and products on the market today that teach the same idea as our product, so why would anyone want to purchase ours? Our book is unlike any other entrepreneur teaching device that you may find on a bookshelf or online. This book will contain information and a guideline about starting a business, along with incorporating true stories from some of the nation's top high school students, which relate to the content in the chapters, about how these seventeen students began and ran a company in under two hundred days.

6.1 Sales Forecast

The following chart and table shows our present sales forecast. We project sales to grow approximately fifty percent the first month and reach maximum for production capacity in May representing sixty-seven percent growth over the previous month.

Sales Monthly

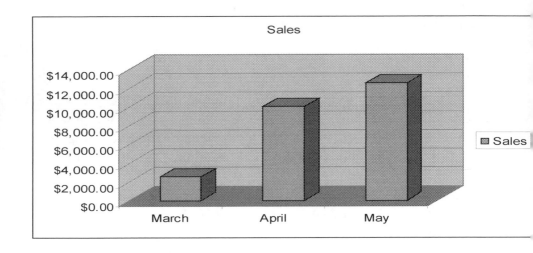

Sales Forecast

	March	April	May
Unit Sales			
Book	100	400	500
Total Unit Sales	100	400	500
Unit Prices	March	April	May
Book	$24.99	$24.99	$24.99
Sales			
Book	$2,499	$9,996	$12,495
Total Sales	$2,499	$9,996	$12,495
Direct Unit Costs	March	April	May
Book	$10.00	$10.00	$10.00
Direct Cost of Sales			
Book	$1,000	$4,000	$5,000
Subtotal Direct Cost of Sales	$1,000	$4,000	$5,000

7. Financial Plan

Start-up Funding

Start-up Expenses to Fund	$5,300
Start-up Assets to Fund	$700
Total Funding Required	$6,000
Assets	
Non-cash Assets from Start-up	$0
Cash Requirements from Start-up	$700
Additional Cash Raised	$0
Cash Balance on Starting Date	$700
Total Assets	$700
Liabilities	
Current Borrowing	$0
Long-term Liabilities	$0
Other Current Liabilities (interest-free)	$0
Total Liabilities	$0
Capital	
Planned Investment	
Investor(s)	$6,000
Additional Investment Requirement	$0
Total Planned Investment	$6,000
Loss at Start-up (Start-up Expenses)	($5,300)
Total Capital	$700
Total Capital and Liabilities	$700
Total Funding	$6,000

7.1 Break Even Analysis

Break-even Analysis	
Monthly Units Break-even	271
Monthly Revenue Break-even	$2,710.00
Assumptions:	
Average Per-Unit Revenue	$24.99
Average Per-Unit Variable Cost	$10.00
Estimated Monthly Fixed Cost	$840.10

THE BOTTOM LINE

A house is never built without a blueprint and a business is never started without a business plan.

Quote From Professional:

"Owning your own business is like a roller coaster-you have your ups and downs with challenges, but always remember to believe in yourself. It speaks volumes." – **Mark Ramsay** President of Golf Range Netting

III. FINANCE

Kaylen James
Chief Financial Officer

* *"The responsibility of the CFO is not for the lazy."*
* *"If you like to take risks and live by your own rules, entrepreneurship is the way to go, but don't be fooled, there is an ugly side."*
* *"In my life, organization has always been a nice habit; however, now I understand it is a necessity in order to fully accomplish anything."*

"In all realms of life it takes courage to stretch your limits, express your power, and fulfill your potential... it's no different in the financial realm." - Suze Orman

Prashant Raju
Director of Finance

* *"The Director of Finance's role is like a child's version of the CFO's."*
* *"The greater the risk, the greater the reward; that's entrepreneurism in a nutshell."*
* *"To most people, starting a company means right away starting a personal business; after taking this course I have learnt the importance of why starting a legal company such as an LLC is needed for personal liability protection."*

"The wheel that squeaks the loudest is the one that gets the grease."
-Josh Billings

Accounting:

"Operating Information" - This is the information that is needed on a day-to-day basis in order for the organization to conduct its business. Employees need to get paid, sales need to be tracked, the amounts owed to other organizations or individuals need to be tracked, the amount of money the organization has needs to be monitored, the amounts that customers owe the organization need to be checked, any inventory needs to be accounted for: the list goes on and on. Operating information is what constitutes the greatest amount of accounting information and it provides the basis for the other two types accounting information.

Financial Accounting Information - This is the information that is used by managers, shareholders, banks, creditors, the government, and the public, to make decisions involving the organization and its operations. Shareholders want information about what their investment is worth and whether they should buy or sell shares, bankers and other creditors want to know whether the organization has an ability to pay back money lent, managers want to know how the company is doing compared to other companies. This type of information would be very difficult to extract if every company used a different system for recording their financial position. Financial accounting information is subject to a set of ground rules that dictate how the information is reported, ensuring uniformity.

Managerial Accounting Information - In order for managers to make the best decisions for their company, they need to have specific information prepared. They use this information for three main management functions: planning, implementation and control. Financial information is used to set budgets, analyze different options on a cost basis, modify plans as the need arises, and control and monitor the work that is being done.

The whole purpose of accounting is to provide information that is useful and relevant for interested parities when making decisions regarding the company and its operations.

In order to do that effectively, a specific language and subsequent rules have been developed for users of the information. By learning accounting you learn these rules and can then communicate financial information with others in a comprehensible and comparable manner.

The most important thing in accounting is an accurate report of where you stand each and every month. Stay on top of all finances; what you've spent, what you've made, and your debt: operating information. Have a plan of what you think you'll make and how much you think you'll need (*Profit and Loss Statement*). Then on a monthly basis compare your active results to your budget. The closer you are to your budget the higher your success. Once you're organized you can begin the ongoing process of financing a business. The easiest way to do this is to set up a spread sheet: place each idea in its given box. Don't forget to add in your taxes and deprecation. Many companies fail to understand this process and end up failing due to their lack of planning for the high taxes. It is also important to hire a CPA who can guide you in your financial decision. Although this will add an extra cost, it reduces the risk of a poor financial decision due to inexperience or lack of financial understanding.

How to Find Banks That Fit Your Needs:

Choosing the best bank for your needs is easy. First, you have to figure out exactly what you need from a bank. Once you know what to look for, you can quickly evaluate the competition and end up with the best bank account out there. This page offers a guide to choosing the right bank for your needs, and offers some ideas for starting your checklist.

* **What Will You Do?**

The fist question to ask yourself is what you want to do with your bank account. Do you want to put money in there periodically and watch it grow? Will you move money in and out quickly? You need to know what your banking behavior will be like in order to find the right bank.

* **How will you do it?**

Next, get an idea of how you prefer to do your banking. If your schedule doesn't work with most bank schedules, the best bank might just be the one that's open at convenient times. If you're a web-savvy customer, look for the banks that make it easy to do your dealings quickly and efficiently with the click of a mouse.

Get Opinions

Finally, remember to ask other people for opinions. You can find bank reviews in our Bank Review pages. Ask your friends where they bank, and how happy they are. Finally, some of the blogs out there have extensive information on customer experiences in banks.

When searching online, just remember that negative experiences will be more common than positive ones. People upset at the bank are motivated to spread the word – but happy customers often don't even realize that they're happy.

Shop Around

Once you know what you want, start shopping and comparing. You can use the list below to start a checklist. Most institutions will have everything you need on their Website. If not, call (or walk in) and ask – you'll get a preview of the customer service. Look for fee schedules, rate sheets, and hours of operation while you're hunting online."

Financing a company is an extensive process. First you must set up a banking account. Your personal credit score is very important in this case. When you start up an account the bank is getting in just as deep as you are. Once you have an account, you can then apply for a loan. The government has accredited the *Small Business Association* to help companies like Lake Highland Entrepreneurs, LLC. The paperwork, however, is extensive and requires a good amount of research and time. If your bank and the government declare your company a good investment they can give you 50-85% coverage of your loan if the company is unable to pay. This has been put into place within the last couple of years to support the success of small businesses, which until now have had numerous failures. Your bank should have many options for you to control your money. Nowadays your account can be monitored online. For Lake Highland Entrepreneurs, LLC we can simply log on to our account from our bank's website and easily see all transactions. Our company was also able to set up a Pay-Pal account corresponding directly to our bank account. The Pay-Pal account allows for customers to purchase online, thus expanding our target market.

Finding investors proves to be a challenging task. For our business, as you can imagine, it was extremely hard to find investors to invest in high school students; however, if your business plan is up to par and the CEO can form a strong relationship with the investor then you are in a much better position to gather investors. People invest in people; therefore, if you earn someone's trust you often earn their business.

For investors you are also able to offer a preferred return on their loans. Our company is projected to offer up to 30% payable interest. Many will think this number is too high for such a small business. However, we only had 5 months and needed the money-- quick and simple; we were going to go big or go home! The interest on these loans will then need to be factored into our expenses. Another way to invest is to purchase stocks. For our business we have decided to have **17** shares and only offer sale in extreme situations such as if we can't pay back our investors or if we need money fast. In order to better understand the stock's worth you must understand the *price earnings (P/E) ratio*. Obviously since we're a new business we have to estimate our P/E ratio by looking at other publishing companies such as Scholastic. We modestly set ours to 3. To find your stock value/earnings per share (EPS), you must multiple the P/E ratio and the earnings per share which can be found by dividing your net profit by the number of shares of stock. If we need money and are forced to sell stocks, we can sell one stock for that x amount depending on our model.

* **Investors:**

Investors act as the fuel that allows each business vehicle to run. They can make or break a company. Attracting investors will require investor presentations. These are held once the business plan is written and the business plan and venture idea as a whole are presented to potential financial contributors. Investor presentations are extremely important and need to be well planned and rehearsed, despite the nerves one can get before or during a presentation. Being prepared and confident are the most important aspects of investment presentations. Remember, anything can happen. If one is prepared and confident in what they have to present, the investors will appreciate the professional qualities of the presentation. This, in turn, will hook them and allow for an investor to find the business venture attractive.

* **For the investors**:

Investment involves staking capital in an enterprise, with the expectation of profit. It is nothing but the use of liquid funds to gain income or increase capital. In order for money to grow, investors need to invest judiciously. There are certain guidelines to be followed to avoid major mistakes.

* **Price of the Company**:

An investor needs to research on the '*Market Capitalization*' of the company he is planning to invest in. It is important to gauge the relative cost of a stock, before making any investments in the company. This can be done by learning the 'P/E Ratio'. P/E ratio refers to the Price is to Earnings Ratio. It is the ratio of a company's current share price to its earnings per share.

Example: If a company is trading at $50 per share and earnings per share over the last 1 year were $ 2 per share, then, P/E ratio for this company's stocks would be $50/$2, that is, $25. High P/E value indicates that the company has high growth prospects in the future.

- P/E ratio can be used to make important investment decisions, by comparing P/E values of various companies.

Is The Company Buying Back Shares: It is very important for investors to observe the per-share growth of a company. A company may not show considerable growth in sales, profit and revenue for a few consecutive years, but could generate large returns for investors by dropping the total number of outstanding shares.

Investment Policy of the Investor: An investor needs to have valid reasons for investing in a particular enterprise. Investment decisions should be solely based on the authenticity of a company. Authenticity, involves the reputation of the company, its management, profits earned, market cap and other such fundamentals related to economics and finance.

Long Term Goals of the Investor: Investment involves risk, but intelligent planning of long-term goals makes investing safe. An investor needs to select a good company that requires him to pay the minimum possible amount initially. He should consider the 'Dollar-cost Averaging Program'.

Dollar Cost Averaging Program: This involves investing a particular amount in the same investment, periodically. Investors need not invest a lump sum amount in a stock all at once. They can invest a little every month in the same stock. Since an investor puts in the same amount of money, he can purchase more shares when the prices are lower. This basically lowers an investor's average cost per share in comparison to the average market price per share, in the same time period. Dollar cost averaging builds the habit of setting aside money for investment. Reinvesting the dividends to grow over a long period of time often proves highly profitable. An investor should look for all valid essentials of an investment before investing.

Budgeting:

Key Points:

- The goal is to make sure your expenses don't exceed your income.
- Start by identifying your income sources and amounts. Then spread these by month based on when you believe the money will be received.
- Once you have your income budgeted you are now ready to budget your expenses.

- You should break your expenses down between those that are fixed each month (i.e. rent, salaries, etc.), those that are variable (i.e. travel, meals, etc.), and the fixed expenses you have to pay no matter how much income you produce. The variable expenses can be reduced or eliminated depending on how much income you produce.
- For each expense category, try to determine a budget amount that realistically reflects your actual expenses while setting targeted spending levels that will also enable you to save money.
- Subtotal the income and expense categories.
- Subtract the total expenses from the total income to arrive at your net income.
- If the number is negative, your expenses are greater than your income. Your situation can probably be greatly improved by changing your spending habits. You should focus on your variable expenses first since these are discretionary.

- If you have a positive net income, you should transfer most of it to a savings or investment account at the end of each month. Extra cash left in a regular checking account has a way of getting spent.
- Once you've got the budgeting process in place, take an in-depth look at your largest spending categories, brainstorm about ways to reduce spending in specific categories, and set realistic goals
- Update your budget and expenses monthly.

Tips:

Don't try to fit your expenses into somebody else's budget categories. Tailor the categories to fit your own situation. Make your categories detailed enough to provide useful information, but not so detailed that you become bogged down in trivial details. Think of your budget as a tool to help you get out of debt and save money, not as a financial diet.

Budgeting goes hand in hand with a well developed Profit and Loss Statement. The act of budgeting simply entails the organization of your finances: profit, cost of goods, and expenses. The hardest part in the budgeting process is including all expenses in the original make-up. This is where one needs to have his or her budget plan reviewed. Although our P&L was reviewed by many, Lake Highland Entrepreneurs, LLC forgot to budget for the cost of the website. Luckily we budgeted for a miscellaneous expense category so our net profit didn't fall. I cannot stress enough how important it is to keep updating the budget plan/P&L. The number of products sold, utility expenses, and new/unexpected cost are in constant motion.

Overview:

Ask yourself: Exactly how are my products and services affecting my business? How much money am I actually making because of those products and services? An income statement answers these and other financial questions. An income statement tells you and any stockholders how your net assets have increased or decreased. On an income statement, the total inflow of net assets resulting from the delivery of services and products to your customers is measured in revenue accounts, which in turn tells you what caused the net assets to increase or decrease.

In addition, you can use a statement of income as a tool to compare the most recent year with past trends, thus forming a reasonable forecast for the future. The statement also helps you locate problem areas regarding sales, margins and expenses, and provides a method for you to investigate problem areas within a reasonable amount of time. When an income statement is prepared properly, the net increase or decrease in your net assets, or the difference between revenue and expense, is designated as net income or net loss. A net increase in net assets or net income is then added to your equity on your balance sheet. This tool examines the process of developing an income statement and explains the meaning of the components of an income statement.

Preparing Profit and Loss Statements:

Let's prepare a profit and loss statement using the sales forecast developed earlier. The sales figures will give us our top line, i.e. the total revenue (or "Gross Revenue") that we might be able to realize if our marketing plan has been successfully implemented. The sales figures themselves ultimately depend on our customers and their propensity to buy our products. However, everything else on the P&L statements is entirely under our management and control. For example, how much we pay our employees, the amount of advertising we do, the efficiency by which we produce our products, etc. are all the result of management decisions we make. A little bit of research (e.g. looking at other companies, making a few phone calls) will quickly give us ranges of values which we can use and work with.

The Cost of Goods sold is what we expect it to cost us to produce those units which we sell in that particular month. This is easy if we outsource, i.e. buy our products from another company. If we make the products ourselves, we will have to carefully analyze our costs, materials, labor, and some overhead allocation. This may entail a completely separate spreadsheet. In this example, we are working on the basis of outsourcing our production requirements. This may increase our direct costs somewhat, but will allow us to keep our indirect, i.e. fixed overhead, costs down initially.

In the "Expenses" category, we have broken our expenses down into three commonly used categories:

- Sales
- Research and Development (R&D)
- General and Administrative (G&A)

Each of these categories should be broken down further into salaries, office costs, rent, utilities, etc. Salaries usually account for the bulk of the expenses in each category. We might even want to show a subtotal for salaries to help us in our planning. It is relatively easy to produce estimates of expenses. These estimates are driven by our marketing mix and how aggressively we wish to build our venture. It is a good idea to do some sanity checks by consulting with peers in your industry. Also, review some statements of publicly listed companies to get additional ideas.

What about equipment and facilities expenditures? Where do these go on a P&L projection? And how do we account for depreciation? Usually on a first-pass projection, you may not go into great detail on equipment and facilities. You could use some monthly rental or lease figures to substitute for equipment or facilities investments. However, depending on the nature of your business, e.g. software vs. hardware, you will undoubtedly have to include these items. Major capital equipment expenditure items belong in the cash flow projections. In the P&L, it would be useful to include any carrying costs, lease or finance costs, as well as depreciation calculations.

The "Total Expenses" line will be very useful to you. Because it is a line that you control almost absolutely, you can very quickly estimate your break-even point (i.e. how long will it take until you start to make a profit), and be able to develop a sense of your "burn rate" - i.e. how much you are spending each month, assuming no revenue from sales. Even though these expenses do not equate exactly to cash flow, they give you a good "feel" for initial cash requirements because you know that these expenses will have to be paid for, either in the current month or the month following.

* **How to Make an Estimate:**

After being in business for a while, it is fairly easy to come up with reliable estimates for expenditures such as salaries, rent, insurance, utilities, and communications costs. When you first begin a venture, how can you easily produce reliable projections? A fairly simple, quick way is to look at the financial statements of similar companies, i.e. similar in size, product type, technology, market, etc. For example, we researched other publishing companies and talked with a few authors who were recently published about their costs. Another way to get some starting figures is to ask around - talk to business people, mentors, etc. and others to get some numbers. It's always a lot better than just guessing.

Each P&L Statement is unique. Obviously different companies are going to have different numbers; however, there are a few sections you should have regardless: Revenue, Cost of

Goods, Expenses, and Net Profit. Within Revenue you should have the cost of your service/product and your estimated (or goal) amount of services/products that will sell. Multiply your cost by total amount sold to find your total revenue. This is your starting amount to pull from and to ultimately calculate the net profit. Next is Cost of Goods which includes the total cost of producing your product or service. For Lake Highland Entrepreneurs, LLC, our cost included the price to publish/print the book, but for a company such as a lawn service, the costs may include the price of gas.

Again, to calculate the total Cost of Goods, you multiply your cost per object with the number of services/products sold.

Expenses are where most companies differ. As you can see in our P&L Statement below, our expenses included: advertising, legal (attorney), accounting (CPA), website, wages, writer, interest on bank loan, interest on investor loan, utilities, and miscellaneous. For the lawn mowing company, their expenses may also include price of mower and price of trailer. As you can see the expense possibilities are endless, so therefore the time you spend gathering the master expense list is key. Total expenses are all expenses added together. Now it is time for the Gross Profit (*EBTDA*): Total Revenue – Total Cost of Goods – Expenses. Unfortunately this is still not pocket cash. The final step is to subtract the taxes. Now what is left is your *Net Profit,* also known as Net Earnings.

EBTDA- "Earnings Before Taxes Depreciation and Amortization" – "EBTDA can be used to analyze and compare profitability between companies and industries because it eliminates the effects of financing and accounting decisions. However, this is a non-GAAP measure that allows a greater amount of discretion as to what is (and is not) included in the calculation. This also means that companies often change the items included in their EBTDA calculation from one reporting period to the next."

Lake Highland Fast Track

P&L Statement

Number of e-Kits Sold	900	
Price per e-Kit	$24.99	
Total Revenue from e-Kits	$22,491	
COST OF GOODS		
Cost Per Handbook	$10	
Total Cost of Handbook	$9,000	40%
EXPENSES		
Advertising	$500	2%
Legal	$500	2%
Accounting	$500	2%
Web Site	$318	
Yearbook	$200	
Writer	$1,000	
Patrick	$500.00	2%
Interest on Loan	$1,800	10%
Utilities	$0	0%
Misc.	$200	1%
Total Expenses	$5,518	25%
Gross Profit (EBTDA)	$7,973	35%
Taxes (Rate 30%)	$2,392	
Net Profit	$5,581	25%

DEBT SERVICE

Loan Balance	$6,000
Bank Loan	$ -
Interest on Loan	30%
Interest Payment	$1,800
Total Debt	$8,300.00

STOCK STRUCTURE

Shares of Stock	17
Earnings per Share(EPS)	$328
Price Earnings Ratio	3
Stock Value	$985
Total Shares	17
Company Value	$16,743
Company Sells for	$16,743
Pay back Loan/Investors	$6,000
Profit after sale	$10,743
Profit per share of Stock	$632

Debt vs. Equity:

In business, loans are taken from investors and banks all the time – but how are they paid back? There are many types of loans, but the two most popular ones are debt and equity.

* **What is Debt?**

Debt is a type of loan where the money borrowed from the investor (or bank) is paid back, but usually with interest. As much as banks and investors want to make a quick profit through the interest of a debt loan, many investors find it risky to give a big loan with debt to a new business because if the company isn't successful and fails to pay back the loan with interest, all the investor or bank can do is foreclose on the company's assets. If the company is a failure then the assets are probably worth nowhere near as much as what the investors lost. Although the percentage of interest on a loan with debt can vary from zero to any amount, the maximum amount of interest, or "usury limit", varies from state to state, but is usually less than 20%. If a company wanted to take a debt loan with 40% in the state of Alabama, where the usury rate is a maximum of 8%, the company would have to take a loan with 8% interest and then have a 32% interest booster.

* **What is Equity?**

Equity is a type of loan that gives stock in exchange for the money from the investors. Investors find equity is even more risky than debt for many reasons, including the most obvious – if the company isn't successful then they owe nothing to the investors or bank and the investors would end up losing quite a bit of money, especially if the company breaks up. However, if the company were successful the investors would make a killing in profit over the period of several years. For example, if a new construction company wanted investors and paid them 10,000 of their 40,000 stock in exchange for $4,000,000, and the company, after 6 years was worth $2,000,000,000 then the investor would end up making way more than he or she put in to the company. The company's total assets minus the company's total liabilities determine the companies' amount of equity.

Debt Equity Ratio:

Since many companies take multiple loans, they have to refer to their loans as the debt equity ratio, which would determine when which loans must be taken to maximize profit and minimize expenses. The equation is total long-term debt divided by the shareholder's equity. The higher the debt equity number, the riskier it is for an investor to invest money in the company. For example if the company has $5,000 percentage in debt loans and $20,000 in equity loans, the debt equity ratio would be .25. If the debt equity ratio is above 1 then the company mainly has been taking out debt loans, and if the number is below 1 then the company has been mainly taking out equity loans.

THE BOTTOM LINE

Business, just like the rest of the world, revolves around money, so always count your pennies. Keep documentation on all purchases. Establish a relationship with your banker and keep your credit score high. People invest in people therefore: be compelling. Stay organized with your finances: revenue, expenses, and cost of goods, by creating a well developed P&L. Pieces of your Company; what it is worth to the rest of the world. Both are loans, but debt is a loan where cash with interest is paid off while equity is a loan where stock is given in place of the money borrowed.

Quote From Professional:

"When you start a business you have to be persistent, creative, and willing to do whatever it takes to get things done" - **Johnnie James** CPA

Maggie Martinez

Chief Marketing Officer

- *"Coming into this class and hearing all the different positions we could have, marketing seemed like the most exciting because it seemed like selling the product and I really thought I would enjoy it...the whole designing of the product and getting people to buy it...but I really didn't have an idea of what it was. I've come to see now that it's more like catering to certain people and manipulating your product to get it to be attractive to the people you are trying to sell it to."*
- *"Entrepreneurialism is something that requires patience, risk and lot of faith in yourself and your ideas. Great success and sometimes great loss... it's a business of extremes"*
- *"Marketing has taught me that life is all about putting yourselves in other people's shoes and being considerate of their interests so they will be drawn to yours"*

Taylor Owen
Director of Marketing

- *"One thing I've learned about Marketing in the business world is that people can be very funny sometimes. They'll spend money they don't have to buy things they don't need to impress people they don't like."*
- *"If you don't know what you're doing, entrepreneurialism can be as complicated as it sounds. A good entrepreneur is one who can not only push past the obstacles and get the job done, but also someone who can spell entrepreneur."*
- *"Life involves risks which can either lead to success or failure. Entrepreneurship only encourages a person to take more of these risks which if done carefully can almost always lead to success."*

Zach Haas
Chief Innovation Officer

- *"Overall, it's been quite an interesting experience. I've acquired so much knowledge about entrepreneurialism, having gone through the process myself. I've worked hard, sat through tedious board meetings, and even met with colleagues outside of school. I'm hopeful that it will all come together."*
- *"The first day I walked into class I just expected it to be an 'easy A' elective, but I had no idea what I was in for."*
- *"The first time I heard the word Chief Innovation Officer, the words stress, brilliant, over-achieving thinker came to mind in my head. But once I settled into the position I discovered that it's a fun and relaxing position with a little bit of power."*

"All your dreams can come true if you have the courage to pursue them"
- Walt Disney

"Authentic marketing is not the art of selling what you make but knowing what to make. It is the art of identifying and understanding customer needs and creating solutions that deliver satisfaction to the customers, profits to the producers and benefits for the stake holders." -Philip Kotler

"Let's not limit our challenges; instead, let's challenge our limits!" -Unknown

Three main points about marketing:

1. You must first analyze what market you are in and come up with an idea that is unique to anything else out there, so you are targeting a market that is unique and that you can successfully compete in.

2. Once you have decided on what your product or service will be you must drive it home to the target market you are catering to; you must advertise in places you know they will be exposed to it and make sure that your product appeals to them specifically.

3. Make sure that your price is competitive as well as your content, find your "niche," making your product unique while still attractive and within the realm of usefulness to your target market. Give your consumers a reason to buy your product or use your service.

Innovation

A Chief Innovation Officer uses his or her own ideas along with a fundamental understanding of marketing and technology to finding the most efficient solution to get a product or idea to the consumer. They develop new ideas, but also recognize innovative ideas generated by other people combining the methods and principles of marketing with technology. To get your product out to your target audience you must challenge the norm and find the newest and most attention grabbing techniques out there. You must always be on the cutting edge and possess the mind of an inventor while being technologically savvy. In this day and age consumers have seen it all and everyone is trying to sell something so they are desensitized to the same old marketing techniques that have been around forever, implementing new modes of advertisement and outlets for getting your product into the public eye is something imperative to stand out against the competition.

Target Market:

* **Demographics:**

Begin your research by checking the demographics of the region that you plan to target. You'll want to know the population's make-up in terms of age, gender, income level, occupation, education, and family circumstances — married, single, retired, and so on. To find that information, you'll probably need to visit the local library. Good sources available at most libraries include:
  * *Country and City Data Book*, published by the U.S. Department of Commerce

  * *Survey of Buying Power Data Service*, published by Sales and Marketing Management

- **Geographic and lifestyle factors:**

Give some thought to where and how your target customers live. Are they Southerners or Yankees; urbanites, suburban soccer moms or country folk? Are they risk-takers or conservative, athletes or couch potatoes, spenders or savers? The answers will help determine what you can sell to them, how you should sell it, and at what price.

No business can be all things to all people. Instead, you must reach specific customers and satisfy their particular needs. As an entrepreneur, you must identify those customers and understand as precisely as possible what they want. The process of finding and studying potential customers for your venture doesn't have to be complex or expensive, but  it is extremely important. In a nutshell, it requires you to find out everything you can about the customers whom you intend to pursue. Once you have that information, you'll have a much better chance of capturing those customers for your business. The facts you need to know about your target market fall into these three categories:

- **Customer needs:**

Consider all of the reasons why people might purchase your product or service. For example, if you're opening a string of health clubs, will your customers come to meet other people, to take exercise classes, or to play racquet sports with their friends?

Find out by talking to people in the local fitness industry and by quizzing friends or acquaintances who go to health clubs. Then you can design and market your club accordingly.

Once you've considered the key demographic factors, you can begin to assemble a customer profile — a more focused statement that describes your target market in detail. Consult that profile when you make decisions about issues such as what products and services to offer or advertise, how much to charge for various products, and expansion plans.

The goal of your market research is to determine your sales demographics and establish a target audience. This is to whom you will gear your advertising and marketing campaign. Just as children's' games and toys clearly state on the box, "for ages 7 through 12," nearly every product or service has a specific demographic group that will be most interested in spending money to buy the product or utilize the services offered. The number of businesses that have failed because the owners have not taken the time to determine their target audience is staggering.

Some products and services, such as selling soda or providing haircuts, will span a wide range of potential customers. Therefore, it is important to create various marketing campaigns to reach the different segments of this vast market that you are most likely to attract. Conversely, other products and services have a narrow audience and need to be targeted in a more specific manner, such as a new service for dermatologists. Niche marketing can be very beneficial and cost effective if done properly.

Some questions to ask yourself when outlining your target market or demographic group include:

- What is the age range of the customer who wants my product or service?

* Which gender would be more interested in this product or service?

* What is the income level of my potential customers?

* What level of education do they have?

* What is their marital or family status?

* Is this a product or service they need or a luxury item?

* How will they use this product or service?

* What will draw them to this product or service? (Easy availability? Low price? Personalized attention? Special features?)

* Which, if any, special features are most appealing?

* What do they like or dislike about the product or service in general?

* Is this an impulse buy or something they are saving up for?

* What is the common method of payment for this product or service? (Cash? Credit Cards? Installment Plans?)

* Where do they gather their decision-making information? (The Internet? Newspapers? Magazines? Books? Television?)

These are just a few of numerous categories in which you can break down your target market.

* Reaching the Consumer

* Effective Advertising

Leahy's Law states that if a thing is done wrong often enough, it becomes right, and as a result, volume becomes a defense to error. When advertising fails to sway consumers, most advertisers follow Leahy's Law by increasing the frequency of the advertising hoping that more of what is not working will somehow work when consumers are subjected to more of the same.

Use the following 10 simple rules to evaluate the advertising you encounter. You may be disappointed, but don't be surprised when you discover that most advertising fails to follow any of the rules.

1.   Does the ad tell a simple story and not just convey information?

A good story has a beginning where a sympathetic character encounters a complicating situation, a middle where the character confronts and attempts to resolve the situation, and an end where the outcome is revealed. A good story does not interpret or explain the action in the story for the audience. Instead, a good story allows each member of the audience to interpret the story as he or she understands the action. This is why people find good stories so appealing and why they find advertising that simply conveys information so boring.

2.   Does the ad make the desired call to action a part of the story?

A good story that is very entertaining but does not make a direct connection between the desired call to action - the purpose of the ad - and the story is just a very entertaining story. The whole point of the story in advertising is to effectively deliver the desired call to action. If the audience does not clearly understand the desired call to action after seeing the ad, then there is no point in running the ad. Contrary to popular belief, having an entertaining story and clearly delivering the desired call to action are not mutually exclusive.

3.   Does the ad use basic emotional appeals?

Experiences that trigger our emotions are saved and consolidated in lasting memory because the emotions generated by the experiences signal our brains that the experiences are important to remember. There are eight basic, universal emotions - joy, surprise, anticipation, acceptance, fear, anger, sadness, and disgust. Successful appeals to these basic emotions consolidate stories and the desired calls to action in the lasting memories of audiences. An added bonus is that successful emotional appeals limit the number of exposures required for audiences to understand, learn, and respond to the calls to action - people may only need to see emotionally compelling scenes once and they will remember those scenes for a lifetime.

4.   Does the ad use easy arguments?

"Jumping to conclusions" literally gave our ancestors an advantage even when the conclusions that made them jump were wrong because delaying actions to review information could have deadly consequences. Easy arguments are the conclusions people reach using inferences without a careful review of available information. Find and use easy arguments that work because it is almost impossible to succeed when working against them.

5.   Does the ad show and not tell?

"Seeing is believing" and "actions speak louder than words" are two common sayings that reflect a bias and preference for demonstrated behavior. This is especially true when interests may not be the same. Assume audiences are skeptical about any advertising and design advertising that shows and does not tell.

6. Does the ad use symbolic language and images that relate to the senses?

People prefer symbolic language and images that relate to the senses. People are far less receptive and responsive to language and images that relate to concepts.

Life is experienced through the senses and using symbolic language and images that express what people feel, see, hear, smell, or taste are easier for people to understand, even when used to describe abstract concepts. The language and images used in advertising should "make sense" to the audience.

7. Does the ad match what viewers see with what they hear?

People expect and prefer coordinated audio and visual messages because those messages are easier to process and understand. Audio and visual messages that are out-of-sync may gain attention, but audiences find them uncomfortable.

8. Does the ad stay with a scene long enough for impact?

People have limited mental processing capacities. Quick cuts to different scenes require people to devote more of their limited resources to following the cuts and fewer resources to processing each scene. It takes people between eight and ten seconds to process and produce a lasting emotional response to a scene. Camera movement or different camera angles of the same scene can engage people through their orienting responses while providing enough time for them to process the scene.

9.   Does the ad let powerful video speak for itself?

Again, the processing capacity of our brains is limited and words may get in the way of emotionally powerful visual images. When powerful visual images dominate - when "a picture is worth a thousand words" - be quiet and let the images do the talking.

10.   Does the ad use identifiable music?

Music can be a rapidly identified cue for the recall of emotional responses remembered from previous advertising.

Making the same music an identifiable aspect of all advertising signals the audience to pay attention for more important content.

How well your advertisements and promotions draw customers will ultimately determine how effective your marketing strategy is. It becomes your responsibility to cultivate your designated market, if you decide to market your invention yourself. One of the ways to do this is through advertising and promotions. Remember the aim of the advertising and promotional strategy is to create awareness of your product, to arouse customers' needs and expectations to the point of consumption and to create a loyal stream of satisfied customers who continue to patronize your business.

Advertising:

The main goal of advertising, as it pertains to marketing, is deciding which forums to advertise your product to so that it is exposed most effectively to your chosen target market. Advertising is a tricky business as you must be attention grabbing while not being obnoxious and pushy or weak and uninteresting. You have to advertise your product with a certain edge, leaving enough to the imagination that the consumers are looking for more after seeing your ad and are encouraged to pursue it.

- **Effective Advertising and Promotions Techniques:**

Perhaps the first step in developing an effective advertising and promotional strategy is to understand the difference between the two concepts. Most people think that advertising and promotions are one in the same; there is, however, a distinction between the two.

While both advertising and promotions use the different media formats - print, radio, and television - as a way of conveying a message, promotion encompasses much more. It is the method of advertising and can entail community involvement.

For example, this could mean sponsoring a Youth Organization, allowing non-profit organizations to use your facility, such as, letting the high school drama club use your parking lot for a car wash fund raiser, sending an underprivileged child to day camp or involvement in any type of positive community activity that will bring attention to your business.

While advertising is a way of keeping your business in the public's eye, promotions are a way of signaling that you are concerned and committed to the welfare of the community and its residents. This commitment may be one of the most effective techniques for building customer loyalty. People tend to be more supportive of businesses and organizations that give something to the community rather than those that just take from the community, never giving anything in return.

Advertising plays an important role in successful business ventures. It entails identifying and selecting the media that provides the greatest amount of exposure for your business and developing effective, yet appropriate materials for each medium.

It is more than running an ad in a local newspaper, on a radio or television station or just simply hanging a sign outside your business and waiting for the customers to purchase your product. It requires that you know your product - that is, the selling points - and that you develop literature that can arouse the customers' consciousness levels to the point that they are curious enough to investigate it, and that raises their need or desire levels to the point that they are willing to purchase it.

Advertising keeps your product or service in the public's eye by creating a sense of awareness. Yet this awareness alone will not ensure the success of your business. Thus, advertising not only has to be effective, it also has to be a continuous process.

It may be a good idea to mix the different media formats that you use. For example, design a brochure that describes your product and emphasize its selling points (special features). Place copies of the brochure in strategic locations of your business to use as customer handouts. Or, devise a customer survey. The survey should focus on whether customers like the product, the quality of the product, ways to improve it, the quality of service provided by staff, and their friendliness and courtesy. Place the survey with a self-addressed, stamped envelope near the check-out counter and ask customers to mail in or return the survey when they come back. Review their comments with staff and implement those suggestions that are practical, cost efficient and can improve the overall quality of service your business provides.

More Media Formats:

Newspaper, radio, or television ads (newspaper advertising is the least expensive and television advertising is the most expensive of these formats). You probably will need professional advice and assistance when developing ads for those media formats. The following media formats you probably can do yourself:

* Business cards
* Classified ads in the local newspaper
* Direct marketing
* Telemarketing (this format can be expensive, also)
* Yellow Pages advertising
* Sampling - mailing or distributing free samples of your product to the public.
* Advertising in community-based magazines or newspapers.

Whatever media format you use, be willing to invest the money needed to develop an effective ad campaign.

Marketing Niche:

* it's more expensive and less profitable to sell a range of products to a lot of people
* be different from your competitors- if not, price will be an issue
* When you decide your niche market you can make your product stand out and cater to a specific audience.
* Make sure when you create a niche that its members have a common interest specific to your niche and different from any other in your industry

- Your product needs to be more appealing to your consumers than the products you are competing against, offer reasons why they should buy yours as opposed to other products
- Make sure your niche is specific but not so specific that it will not be able to generate the revenue you want
- Find the most obvious niche you can whose members aren't already being targeted.

By constantly looking at your competition and assessing the market, you will have a better idea of what you need to do to redirect your focus and concert your efforts so that they are most effective. You must test your unique idea in open forums of discussion as well as test market with possible consumers. In the end it is they who decide how well your product or service does. The fact that you think it is a good idea has little to do with its actual success. categories:

Give your Consumers something to talk about:

- Truly great products sell themselves and get people talking
- If you create a product that is truly interesting, useful and is something that people can actually use then they will talk about it and it will be a way of selling itself.
- Advertising a product worthy of praise is a much easier task than trying to sell something that you know deep down isn't worth its weight.
- However, if you product does take off you must remember that the reason for its success was its versatility and appeal to the consumers and you must therefore always be looking for ways to improve or mold your product to the ever changing times, trends and economy.

Marketing Environment:

Understanding your Marketing environment is imperative to creating a unique and competitive product or service. You must know what else is out there so that you can most effectively compete or set yourself apart from it. You are compared to every last detail  from price to content and it is, therefore, extremely important for you to be, "aware of your surroundings," so that you may ensure the success of your product or service. Every so often it is important to look at the big picture. Look at who your consumers are and who your competition is.

The four P's of marketing – Product, Pricing, Place, and Promotion:

- Consumer market- who you are trying to make your product appeal to
- Answer these questions: What products will be offered? Who will be the target customers? How will the product meet those customers? Why will customers prefer our products to those of our customers?
- Marketing is a societal process which discerns consumers' wants, focusing on a product or service to fulfill those wants, attempting to move the consumers toward the products or services offered.
- Marketing is fundamental to any businesses growth. The marketing teams (marketers) are tasked to create consumer awareness of the products or services through marketing techniques.

- Unless it pays due attention to its products and services and consumers' demographics and desires, a business will not usually prosper over time.

Quote from professional:

"I try to keep up with all the new products on the market and new ideas so I can incorporate them into my designs." Sam Bhikha Commercial/Residential Construction

Business Style and Etiquette:

Quotes:

- *"For us, as high school students in business, people are bound to ask questions, but there's no time for that, we have no room for mistakes or being unprofessional."*
- *"Robert's Rules turned a classroom full of unorganized high school kids into a boardroom full of on-task business professionals."*
- *"You want to be what everyone's talking about, but for the right reasons; you want admiration and respect, not scandalized whispers."*

Three Points to Style:

- Dressing for Success
- Robert's Rules of Order
- Professional Attitude

- **Dressing Professionally:**

The way you present yourself and what you wear in the business world is of the utmost importance in how you are treated and in the respect will receive from those you interact with. The term, "dress for success," is one of the most literally applicable sayings in the English language. Professional dress is more about being subtle than standing out; you want to make a statement, but not one that warrants unwanted attention. You want people to know you are ready to get down to business while making it look effortless at the same time. It is incredibly important to know how dressy or casual to go when you have an appointment, meeting, party, or business lunch Being underdressed is never okay; so when in doubt err on the side of more rather than less; nobody will ever reprimand you for being the only person wearing a tie.

For men, your suit needs to be well-tailored and your tie properly tied. Your shirt and tie, if you are wearing one, should complement each other and not clash or be overwhelming. Your shoes, belt, glasses and cufflinks should match and look as if they were made to go together. You should be wearing an outfit, not a chaotic mixture of random accessories that are filling a missing space. These small things may seem tedious and overly nitpicky, but to a successful businessperson, these are a necessity. You can be sure they will be noticed.

For women the most important thing to be aware of is looking appropriate; sky-high hem length, super tight fabrics, and low-cut shirts should be something kept far from the working world for many reasons.

Wearing something inappropriate is an easy way to lose the respect of everyone you are working with and can oftentimes take away from great ideas you have to offer. Besides being appropriate you want to look well put together, and just like men, your clothing should fit well, not too small, but not too big either; it should, again, be noticed but not the topic of conversation. For both men and women the way you dress is a way to express yourself and show off your own personal style, but the best way for your creativity to be appreciated is if you start with an appropriate foundation and then add in the little accents that reflect who you are!

In the end, business is all about relationships and to forge those relationships you have to market yourself to others by being appropriate, well put together and looking sharp.

- **Professional Attitude:**

Your attitude and the way you interact with co-workers and clients is very important to the relationships you make with them and the amount of trust they are willing to put in your hands. You must know what you are talking about and be confident; look  people in the eye and give them the impression that you genuinely care about what they are telling you, regardless of how little you

- **Robert's Rules of Order:**

Robert's Rules of Order is one of the oldest and most effective ways to maintain command in a professional environment.

Robert's Rules are efficient and ensure that no time is lost with petty chatter that does nothing but detract from the ideas and the progress being made. It makes sure that all ideas are heard and that no rash decisions are made in the heat of the moment.

It covers everything from making group decisions to the correct way to voice your opinion so that it is appropriate and heard by all in the group. It levels the playing field guaranteeing the person with the least status shares the same amount of representation and voice as the most powerful person in the group. It is a system that can be used for everything from something as small as a Student Government meeting to a board meeting for one of the largest banking firms in the country.

Business relationships are completely reciprocal. You will get out of it what you put in. If people get the sense that you care about what they have to say then they will invest the same interest in what you have to offer. Exude an appearance of complete self-assurance in yourself and your ideas no matter how outlandish they might seem. The difference between crazy ideas and genius is proper delivery. Work on your weaknesses. Even if you have a great personality, if you don't have, for example, a firm handshake, it's a strike against you and will detract from your strengths. Being polite and having a good attitude, no matter what you are feeling, is incredibly important when you are making business agreements, deals and transactions.

Your vocabulary is also important. One slip of the tongue can sometimes be the deal breaker for a potential client or new boss. Even if the most important person in the room is swearing like it's his job in life, let him look like a tasteless fool and maintain your refined composure. You never know whom you might offend. Be efficient and on the ball. Make sure everyone around you sees you as someone who gets the job done and someone who takes great responsibility even in times of stress or pressure. Don't intimidate, rather, command respect while giving the impression that you are approachable and easy to talk to.

How you present yourself in business is directly related to the amount of respect you receive from your bosses, clients, and colleagues. First impressions are everything. The way you present yourself when you first meet somebody is of the utmost importance.

THE BOTTOM LINE

Marketing requires confidence and innovation. It takes a feeling or even a gutsy impulse of just putting your ideas out on the line hoping for success. Constant improvement is an utter necessity as new ideas are always flowing, each new idea seeming better and more exciting than the last. The customer isn't always going to come to you; you need to figure out how you can reach them and reaching them is imperative to effectively marketing what you are trying to sell.

Taylor Greenip
Art Director

- *"Being the Art Director lets me help give a face to the company… and I don't have to deal with numbers."*
- *"Entrepreneurship is an occupation that can have major ups and downs, but that helps make it one of the most interesting occupations you can have."*
- *"As the Art Director I'm able to see the application of art in a business setting rather than in just a purely artistic setting."*

"We would accomplish many more things if we did not think of them as impossible." -Vince Lombardi

Uniqueness:

Most importantly, whatever you have designed or design yourself must stand out and be unique. The job of the Art Director is essentially to make the product and the company itself stand out visually.

Clarity:

You don't want people to have to figure out what one of your designs is. It has to be clear and obvious. Many corporate logos are very simple so people won't have trouble recognizing them.

Color:

Make sure you are using the right colors for what you're trying to accomplish. Different colors give off different subtle connotations. For example, a hard red means action and authority while a pastel blue gives more of an idyllic feeling.

Graphic Design:

Graphic design is key to giving your business a face among the public. For example, what picture comes to mind when you think of MasterCard? Two intertwining circles. That is their corporate logo and it was designed by a graphic designer. But that is not all a graphic designer does. A book cover, an album cover, a magazine ad, and a business card are all things made by graphic designers. A skilled graphic designer can help you sculpt your business look to your liking. Graphic design is all about communicating an idea to the viewer whether it's with an image, words, or a combination of the two. Graphic designers know how to use images to help convey certain emotions and feelings and use this skill in all of their work.

Creativity:

Creativity is important as ever in business. It can determine if your business is wildly successful or an embarrassing failure. Creativity is directly linked to innovation. New things and new ideas come from creative people, things a successful business should always be looking for. Being creative is a sure way to get yourself noticed.

Sometimes a creative edge can give you an advantage over your competition. Sometimes that may be all you have to go on. In the future, when today's developing countries become developed, American businesses will have to rely increasingly upon creativity and innovation because these countries will have much more manpower than the United States.

THE BOTTOM LINE

The Art Director is responsible for giving a fresh innovative look to your product, service or company. They must assess the interests of the consumer and work with the marketing department to creating something that is aesthetically appealing.

Quote from Professional:

"Our firm's key to success was hiring the right people, empowering the staff to make decisions, and always putting the needs of our clients superior to the needs of our firm." -Bill Maroon President of Maroon Fine Homes

Josh Korshack
Director of Public Relations

- *"I dream that I can one day be a successful sports agent so frankly, at first, I had no interest in Public Relations, but after my experience in Public Relations I have realized that it has everything to do with being a sports agent and selling your product. Public Relations has now grown on me; it no longer seems like a tedious task but rather a fun and educational experience."*
- *"I feel that the entrepreneurship skills that I have learned in this class have given me a tremendous head start and the abilities to start my own sports agency one day."*
- *"I think that my perspective has changed because if 17 kids can do it I'm pretty sure anyone can."*

Jaymee Leffler
Director of Public Relations

- *I feel the role of Public Relations is a significant and powerful one, of which I was previously unaware. As Director, I am given control over the writing of press releases and newsletters that have the potential of reaching thousands of interested buyers. I am also a part of managing the database of all our prospective customers and target markets. The many responsibilities that come along with being Director have opened my eyes to the world of advertisement and the significant effect of press releases on the company's sales.*
- *"Entrepreneurialism is a brave and courageous occupation and undertaking. You are required to have more motivation*

and drive to push yourself to be better than the competitor than most other jobs would find necessary. Yet, when successful, the rush is ever more exciting than any corporate job position in a chain company. The requirements are many but the rewards are endless."

* *"The Director of Public Relations is a role which gives you a greater confidence with people and the skills that come with holding meaningful conversations with interested customers. I have learned the important tactics of making the product appealing and advertising worthy to audiences of different interests. I believe the benefits of being a part of this field are innumerable and will be sufficiently useful in all aspects of life."*

"Failing to prepare is preparing to fail." -John Wooden

Cameron Tallon
Director of Public Relations

* *"As a Director of Public Relations, my job involves crafting a positive image of Lake Highland Entrepreneurs LLC and making sure this image is viewed by the community. After receiving the job as a Director of Public Relations, my level of involvement substantially increased."*

* *"Public Relations are a management function which tabulates public attitudes, defines the policies, procedures and interest of an organization followed by executing a program of action to earn public understanding and acceptance." – Edward Bernays.*

* *"As a Public Relations Director it is important for creating and maintaining particular relationships with media sources and accounts which are beneficial for a company's success."*

85

David Maguire
Director of Public Relations

Three Points Concerning PR:

1. **Be Congenial:** By going out, meeting people, making contacts, and by just being a friendly person you can build various connections with powerful people.
2. **Be Concise:** Whether you are writing a press release or just referencing your product by mouth, be concise. It makes you seem bolder and more confident about your product, and it will impress those around you.
3. **Be Persistent:** Mark Hayes taught me to be persistent if you really want something because people will appreciate your determination.

Writing a Press Release:

Writing a press release is not as hard as it is made out to be. It might be the most important part in selling your product as it can either make or break it. If you don't think you can handle the stress of writing a press release, you can hire a company to write it for you but first you must get some simple facts together: you need your company's mission statement, "a summary describing the aims, values, and overall plan of an organization or individual" (Dictionary.com), you need a short and concise sentence to sell your product and a long yet concise paragraph to sell your product, you need a summary about what your company is and what it does/has done, and then a logo. We would have to say that the best way to writing a press release when running your company is to hire a company to do it for you. The fact is that the company will make more money in the long run if your time is used efficiently, and you will actually save money by hiring a company to write the press release for you and alleviating the task of writing it yourself.

Our Press Release: Jessi Blakley, Consensus Communications

LAKE HIGHLAND SENIORS' NEW BUSINESS MAKES MONEY, HISTORY

ORLANDO, Fla.; May 24, 2008 — When 16 seniors at Lake Highland Preparatory School decided to sign up for the school's first Entrepreneurship class, little did they know their small company would be successful, profitable or even historical.

Under the direction of Bob Vander Lugt and Program Chairman and local businessman Mark Hayes, the enterprising partners founded Lake Highland Entrepreneurs, L.L.C. with a mission to successfully create, operate and sell a company during the 18-week semester.

Led by CEO Will Maddux, CFO Kaylen James and COO Adam Maali, the savvy seniors developed a strategic business plan, with heavy emphasis on promotional, marketing and public relations activities that has launched their small business into the limelight.

Proving that education can be much more than a class, Lake Highland Entrepreneurs developed a package to teach new entrepreneurs the skills and knowledge they need to successfully start and run their own business. Mapping out their journey in an autobiography titled "Entrepreneurship: The Bottom Line," the seniors share their secrets to entrepreneurial success alongside those of other local entrepreneurs in an inspiring, back-to-basics guide to business.

Pre-sales of "Entrepreneurship: The Bottom Line," are currently available through the company's Website, www. lakehighlandentrepreneurs.com for only $24.99.

"As an entrepreneur and local business owner, it's been really amazing to watch these kids grow and transform into business men and women in only a few weeks," said Hayes. "Their level of knowledge and incredible drive for success is what I hope will drive the next generation of business leaders."

In addition to Maddux, James and Maali, Lake Highland Entrepreneurs is operated by a team that includes Alexis Charran, Taylor Greenip, Graham Grindstaff, Mark Jensen, Nick Keener, Josh Korshak, Jaymee Leffler, Blake Maher, Maggie Martinez, David McGuire, Taylor Owen, Prashant Raju, and Cameron Tallon.

In addition to online sales, the organization plans to host a variety of book sale events both on and off of Lake Highland's campus.

Lake Highland Entrepreneurs, L.L.C. was established in 2008 by an entrepreneurial group of 16 Lake Highland Preparatory high school students with a mission to successfully create, operate and sell a company in less than five months. The scholarly effort was created to enable student's hands-on experience and knowledge in the development and implementation of starting a business. Lake Highland Entrepreneurs hopes to inspire other hopeful entrepreneurs, leading by example, and showing others that the seemingly impossible can and has been achieved. For more information, please contact www.lakehighlandentrepreneurs.com.

THE BOTTOM LINE

Public Relations is all about first getting a handle on what your product is so that you can successfully advertise it to the public working with those around you to present your product/service in the best possible light. It then involves finding different outlets to expose your idea to the market it was meant to reach.

Quote from professional:

"I think a key to our success is that we started small and kept our expenses to a minimum until we could afford more things. We did not borrow today leaving tomorrow to pay for it" –Johnnie James CPA

Graham Grindstaff
Account Executive

* *"When you are going after some big "fish," you have to have the right bait ready before you try to catch them."*

Mark Jensen
Director of Sales

The three most important things to have are good communication skills, knowledge of the subject, and hard work/persistence. Your physical and verbal presentation when speaking with a buyer are both key factors. You must look professional as well as sound professional. It is important that you are confident in the product you are trying to sell and are outgoing about how good the product is. It is good to be very detailed and knowledgeable in your presentation, but precise at the same time. You don't want to drag out a sales meeting but want to show them you know your product like the back of your hand and can answer any question they throw at you. It is said that hard work and persistence are the two most important things in salesmanship.

Some believe that any body who has got moderate intelligence, moderate selling skill but is hard working will be successful. You have to be able to go out of your comfort zone and really express how you feel about your specific product and be persistent with the buyer, pretty much doing whatever it takes (legally and ethically) to get their business.

The price of a product is an important aspect for a company trying to land among the 2% of small successful businesses in America. The idea of product or service is the drive and motivation for any company. If we didn't have an innovative thought of some sort of product that could  potentially sell, why would anyone even think to start a company? Therefore, a product and its likelihood of success is crucial to any business big or small. noticed.

When valuing your product, you must consider your competition, your target market, and your cost of goods along with other underlying cost. Knowing your competition is important in order to make sure your price is reasonable. Comparing your product's physique, such as its quality, design, and internal information, to other similar products plays a role in putting a price tag on your product. The target market is important to study simply because if you are aiming for teenagers or young adults, it is likely that they do not have as much "loose change" or extra spending cash lying around as an age group of people who have a reliable income. Many companies get crushed and sent down the road of failure simply because of the nickels and dimes they forget about here and there. Companies tend to fail because they are not making as great of a profit as they originally planned, simply because they forgot about basic costs such as storage or energy. Pricing a product is the combination of research and mathematics to equate the perfect price tag to reach the maximum amount of sales.

Valuing a product or service can be the difference between a company being a failure or becoming wildly successful.

Salesmanship:

Salesmanship is not as complicated as most people think. There is a simple art to it… Treat people with respect. When you are going to buy a car you do not like it when people ride you and try to force you to buy a car. The same goes for everything. Even when I'm looking for clothes I feel very uncomfortable when people are following me around asking if I want their help.

Once you have caught the fish by the hook you have to do the right work to reel them in. You must know the product inside and out, you have to be confident with your words, you have to be patient and, again, you must treat people with respect.

* **Accountability**:

Sure, completing the product was difficult and time consuming but selling the product is what makes your company its money. Everybody on your team is counting on you at this point and it is up to you to make the sales. You also have to make it easy for the account reps you are dealing with to get in contact with you. You are the only person in the company they know and they have probably created a form of trust in you.

- **Perseverance**:

You are not always going to make the sales that you hope to make. When this happens you have to be able to get back up and try again. There are people out there that want your product. Do not become discouraged by your team, your product, or, most importantly by yourself. Your team is counting on you and you need to keep trying. Maybe go after a smaller "fish" first and then work your way up.

Sales Plan:

A sales plan is your strategic and tactical plan for achieving your marketing objectives. It is a step-by-step and detailed process that will show how you will acquire new business and how you will gain more business from your existing customer base. It involves making and/or exceeding your sales quota within your sales territory. The key feature of sales plans is its use of unit projections and associated dollar values. Sales plans are about targets and numbers. The first step is to clearly identify your target markets. If you are targeting several markets, the next step is to prioritize your target market to ensure that your resources are directed towards your key target market.

- **Developing a Sales Strategy:**

Your sales strategies will include determining how you can reach your sales quota, how you can get more sales from existing customers, and how you can raise awareness in the marketplace and in your community about your business. Your sales strategies also involve making a decision on who is actually going to do the selling.

* **Building a Team:**

A Business team is made up of many different people with many different skills but with all of their eyes focused on the same goal. The most important of these people is the Chairman of the Company. This person is the Primary owner of the Business. The next on the line of important people are the officers: the CEO, the COO, and the CFO. The CEO is the highest person on the pole other than the chairman. CEO stands for Chief Executive Officer. The CEO is the one the runs the company and makes the final decisions before something is sent to the Chairman. COO stands for Chief Operating Officer. The COO is the one that keeps the company going; the COO knows what every single person is doing that is involved with the company. The COO is the CEO's right hand man. CFO stands for Chief Financial Officer. The CFO is the person that is in charge of all the money that is made and spent. This person must be great with numbers, and hopefully have some knowledge of computer science.

After the Officers there are the Directors. There is a Director of Sales, Marketing, and Administration. The Director of Sales, along with his or her team of workers, is in charge of getting the sales number, the estimates, and the sales pitch completed. The Director of Marketing, along with his or her team, is in charge of marketing the product and getting the product advertised with the given budget. The Director of Administration is in charge of making the rules of the company. Finally the rest of the people in the company do what they are told to do by their director. These people are on certain teams and help their director get their team's task completed.

* **Finding the consumer:**

Getting your business recognized amidst the hustle and bustle of the free market is no easy feat. Even if you have invented a completely unique product, there is no guarantee you'll get noticed by anyone. A deliberate and well-focused marketing plan can help you do just that. By following several age-old marketing principles, you and your business will realize both recognition and profitability.

* **Identify Your Customer Profile:**

Blanket e-mails to thousands of recipients and mass mailings to entire communities rarely hit the mark when it comes to advertising. It just doesn't make sense to waste your hard-earned money vying for the attention of disinterested customers. By defining your target customers, you'll be able to more precisely market to them.

There are a myriad of methods for identifying your target market. Begin by listing the projected qualities of the types of customers you think will be interested in your product. Once you've solidified an initial profile, get out amongst these people and get their reactions to your product. Hold focus groups, send out surveys, and ask for people's honest opinion of your product. This will not only help you figure out who wants to buy your product, it'll also help you make improvements based on their feedback.

Submitting several press releases is a great jumping-off point. A press release is a written piece highlighting your business and the unique service or product you have to offer. It is wise to avoid fluffy marketing language, while keeping it engaging. Oftentimes press releases will feature a brief background of the company and its products. It is also common to include a quote or two from those involved in the business. A direct quote from the owner can give some extra credibility to the content.

- **How to Get Noticed:**

The methods through which a company can market are endless. Television commercials, radio, sports, newspaper advertisement and billboards first come to mind. In the case of a new business, it is best to start small and build on subsequent successes.

Another necessary element of any business' marketing strategy is a good website. If you have some expertise in creating web pages, you may be able to take care of the entire thing yourself. Many, however, choose to hire a web designer to help make the site appear more professional. In the eyes of consumers, a professional looking website with useful and informative content means a solid product and a reliable company. Continue to manage your site and make sure someone at your company can be easily reached. Once your website is in working order, you can start taking advantage of other marketing opportunities on the Internet. Participating in public forums and hosting a blog are both great ways to directly communicate with customers while simultaneously gaining name recognition.

Writing articles and submitting them to online article databases is another way to gain an identity for your business on the Internet. These databases distribute your articles to hundreds of sites to be published along with a link back to your own website. You might as well attract some traffic to that site you worked so hard on!

There are numerous methods that companies use to achieve that highly sought after brand recognition. By creating an effective marketing plan and following through with the aforementioned promotional opportunities, you will be well on your way to getting recognized.

Presentation:

- **Overview and Objective of the Presentation:**

Product presentations are an important part of selling your product to prospective customers. In many cases, this will be the customer's first introduction to your company and potentially your product. First impressions are critical. There are also times when it is important to sell your product to the people inside your company as well as investors. Proper preparation is vital to presenting your product in the best light possible.

The objective of the product presentation is different depending upon the target audience and the presentation should be adjusted accordingly. It is important to know your audience and why they are interested enough to hear your presentation.

- **Points to Consider:**

Before you even start building your presentation, be sure you know the following information:

- **Objective/call to action** - At the end of your product presentation you want something to happen, either you want a customer to move forward to evaluate your product, your management to buy into what you are doing with the product, your sales people eager to sell your product, or an investor or your management to provide additional funding of your product.

* **Target audience** – To whom are you giving the presentation? (Prospective customers, investors, management). What is their industry like right now? What are their needs and immediate concerns? What are their individual goals? Where is their pain?

* **Orientation** - How much does your audience know of your product and other similar products? What is special about the way this audience looks at your product? Do they have any preconceived notions? Are they looking at your competitors? If so, which ones? What are their special interests?

* **Target presenter** - Who will be giving the presentation (you, sales person, company executive)?

It is helpful to write the above information down before building the product presentation so that you can go back and review it if you get stuck on any given point. You will want to refer to it later to make sure the presentation meets the objective and you will also need it for doing practice runs.

Once you have your basic product presentation, it can be modified for other presenters and other audiences, but it is important to have a target audience and a target objective when building the initial presentation. Failure to do so can result in a presentation that doesn't speak to the audience and one that is not focused on their needs.

* **Outline of the Product Presentation:**

The following is a basic outline for a product presentation. You will note that the maximum number of slides is twenty. Most sales calls allow 30 minutes for the formal presentation, at two minutes a slide, fifteen slides is the appropriate number. It is important to keep your presentation precise otherwise your point will be drowned out in detail.

1)   **Introduction** - This is normally just a title slide where the speaker introduces themselves, and the point of the product presentation. This is where you want to hook your audience and tell them what is in it for them. If you are not going to be giving the presentation you may want to have a note slide with the point on it. (1-2 slides)

2)   **Agenda** - An agenda is optional, but provides you with an opportunity to tell your audience what you are going to cover in your presentation. It avoids people asking questions early in the presentation about material you will be covering later. (1 slide)

3)   **Company Information** - This is a way to establish credibility and to make the audience feel comfortable with your company. Ways to do this include customer lists, high-profile executives or advisors, information on funding (if a private company), awards and major milestones. Don't spend too much time on this; you don't want your audience falling asleep.

4)   **Positioning** - Successful products have a unique technology or positioning that sets them apart from other products on the market. You want to introduce this aspect of your product up front to let your audience know how your product is different and why they should listen to the rest of your presentation. Use this as an attention getter. This should be done in terms of the problem that they have and that you are solving with your product. Be sure to present this in terms of your audience and their pain. Performing a positioning exercise prior to building your presentation is very helpful. This part of your presentation must be very crisp and to the point. (1-5 slides)

5)   **Product description** - Clearly describe your product in terms that your audience will understand. It may be helpful to have a chart with the product components. You want to give the audience a frame of reference for the features and benefits that they are going to see. You also want them to know how your product fits into their existing environment. Show how the product interfaces with other products or systems they may be using. (1-2 slides)

6)   Clearly articulated benefits as they relate to your target audience - You can use a features and benefits list or just walk through the features and benefits. Whatever you do, do not forget the benefits. They may be obvious to you because you live and breathe the product, but your audience should have them clearly called out and they must relate to their needs. (1- 5 slides)

7)   Examples/successes - At this point in the presentation your audience should be familiar with your product and why it is different and better. In order to drive this point home use examples of how your product is being used and how customers have benefited from the product. (1-3 slides)

8)   Closing argument - This is your opportunity for a 'call to action'. You want summarize your product presentation, reiterate the point of the presentation, and ask your audience to do something, if that is the point of your presentation.

Other Important Points:

•Use Examples:

Use examples whenever possible. Examples help to illustrate your points and provide a frame of reference for those people in your audience that don't already have one.

- **Simplify:**

Keep slides as simple as possible. Lots of text on a slide makes it difficult to read and it loses its impact. Make sure the slides will be readable from the back of the room. If you are not giving the presentation, you may feel compelled to add more text to the slides - provide speaker's notes instead.

If you are using PowerPoint, don't get carried away with colors and many different transitions. Pick a format and stick with it so that you don't draw attention away from your subject.

Provide Handouts:

You will probably hand out copies of the slides. It is always nice to print the slides in a format where there is room for the audience to take notes.

One of the most effective presentations that I ever saw was done with a single clip-art picture in the middle of each slide. The picture makes a point without drawing attention away from the speaker.

- **Easy-to-Read Fonts:**

A san-serif font (a font that does not have the little lines at the top and bottom, as in the headings of this document) is easier to read for bullets on slides.

* **Style:**

A presentation that uses the default PowerPoint fonts and lots of different primary colors looks like a presentation that was slapped together with little thought. Not everyone is a graphic artist, but you can learn some basic principles and apply them to your slides. Below are a few key points.

Use a presentation template and then use the colors from the template (or ones in the same family) for all charts and graphs. Use alignment carefully. If your template is left or right aligned, use that alignment throughout the presentation.

Remove harsh lines. PowerPoint always puts a dark line around any box that you draw. These lines make the drawings look crude and harsh. By removing the lines your eye focuses more on the content of the box rather than the boxes themselves. Additional lines and arrows don't have to be dark either; try making them thicker and lighter so that they don't draw attention away from the point of the slide.

* **Provide Speaker's Notes:**

In order to keep the bullets on your slides concise; you may want to consider providing speaker notes to people that may be giving your presentation. If you do provide these notes, keep them short and concise and use bullets to make it easy to read. Remember that the more text you put on the speaker's notes, the less likely the speaker is to read it before the presentation.

If you are using PowerPoint, print the slides with the speaker's notes so that the presenter does not get the notes out of sync with the presentation.

You may want to use handouts in addition to providing copies of the slides. Often, to keep slides simple, you may compromise the ability for the viewer to use it as a reference later or you may have charts or back-up information that has too much detail to include in your presentation. In these cases it may help to include handouts and refer to them during your presentation.

⁕ **Use Themes for Group Presentations:**

If there are a group of people presenting it is helpful to use a theme and weave it throughout all the presentations. This provides a sense of cohesiveness to the entire presentation.

A good agenda is an important part of group presentations. You want to introduce all the speakers and let the audience know the topic each speaker will be discussing.

⁕ **Mark Confidential:**

If the presentation is confidential, don't forget to mark it confidential. Slides often get copied at customer sites and can easily end up in your competitors' hands.

- Your pitch will be more powerful, polished, and professional
- You are more likely to accomplish your objective
- You look better

There is nothing worse than watching a presenter bring up a slide and then try to interpret it as if this is the first time they are seeing it. The slides are to support your presentation. I will often give the presentation to a practice audience within the company first before giving it to an external audience. You will get some great suggestions from people who have a slightly different perspective. This is especially true if you can give your pitch to a different department. I have found that giving a product presentation to the engineering group will provide some great insights. Before you give your presentation to a practice audience, be sure to go over the "Points to Consider" above with your audience so that they understand your objective, target audience, and that target audience's perspective.

Additionally you should add slides that talk specifically to your audience. Identify the issues and problems that they are dealing with or tell them about how their competition is doing something. Then show them how your product will provide them with a competitive advantage.

Other helpful hints:

- Use gestures to make things visual and clear.
- Use an expressive voice to emphasize points and show your enthusiasm for your product.
- Always stand, even when you are talking to a small audience. Standing projects more energy.
- Use highlights or colors on charts to emphasize an important point. (Though don't over use this, and don't use red unless you want to set off alarms.)

105

- Use controversy - It is sometimes useful to start your presentation with a controversial statement to grab your audience's attention.
- Use metaphors to help with visualization.
- Make sure you have a smooth verbal transition between slides for a very polished presentation. (This is where the practice really pays off.)

Negotiation:

When your business has no revenue and you have very little negotiating leverage beyond the power of your business idea, the traditional rules of negotiation just don't apply. Here are some tips for the entrepreneur who's faced with the prospect of negotiating with employees, investors and suppliers during the startup stage.

Negotiating With Employees:

In a previous column, we discussed how to hire and pay employees during the startup stage when you can't afford to pay market-level wages. Inevitably, however, your employees and consultants will be faced with a need for more money and will knock on your door to negotiate a better deal. How should you handle this situation?

First, you should always be respectful of the personal needs of your employees. In a small startup that's resource-constrained, employees' personal lives and professional lives are particularly intertwined. This doesn't mean giving employees a raise if they ask for it, but it does mean listening carefully to the reason for their request for more money. In many cases, they may not need more money but simply more flex time, more vacation, more upside potential, more downside protection, more respect or more inspiration. Most employees--and especially consultants--won't tell you the real reason for their request unless you ask them repeatedly in different ways to describe why they're really asking for a raise.

When negotiating compensation, it's best to link employee pay with company performance rather than just link it to employee performance during the startup stage. This puts pressure on the business model to work--so everyone gets paid--and it puts pressure on team members to hold each other accountable, because their compensation is linked to each other's performance.

The downside of this incentive structure is that you may have a top-performing employee who doesn't get a salary increase or bonus because of execution problems among his or her colleagues. You should deal with this on a case-by-case basis and may want to provide occasional bonuses for exceptional performance. In practice, giving employees a gift certificate for a trip or an expensive dinner out for their family and friends may provide a better incentive than a cash bonus pool that becomes the source of tension among employees. In a small startup, a cash bonus pool to be divided among employees is a bad idea and undermines the base compensation levels you've negotiated with them.

* **Negotiating With Investors:**

Traditional negotiation theories tell you to understand your BATNA--or Best Alternative to a Negotiated Agreement--before you begin negotiations. Unfortunately, for most cash-strapped startups seeking capital from investors, your BATNA is going out business! So a negotiation theory for startups requires a different approach. Here are some tips for negotiating with investors when your BATNA is closing shop and going back to a 9-to-5 job:

1.   Never let them see you sweat. Investors will only put money in a company if the entrepreneur is confident of the company's prospects. They might know you have few alternatives for startup financing, but when they see your confidence, they'll temporarily forget about those other options.

2.   Draft the investment terms before the meeting. It might be putting the cart before the horse, but it's critical to have investment terms clear in your head before you meet with investors. If you're pitching venture capital investors, get familiar with term sheets before you walk in the door. If you're raising money from relatives, friends or other business angels, read this column for tips on how to make the pitch and structure the investment options.

3.   Tell minority investors that you have standard terms that are non-negotiable. Don't let investors restructure your investment terms unless they plan to lead the entire round of fundraising. Most investors will actually prefer you to have standard terms so they can focus on evaluating the business proposition rather than the investment terms. Avoid the temptation to negotiate individual terms with each investor because it will likely cause you headaches down the line when certain investors are paid back before others.

• Negotiating With Suppliers:

During the startup stage, it's almost always a problem to negotiate favorable deals with suppliers. How can you strike a deal for a volume discount when you can't accurately forecast sales volume? How can suppliers provide you with credit when you don't have a track record with other suppliers?

We recommend negotiating with suppliers just like you'll negotiate with investors: Put your best foot forward, and let them believe in your company as much as you do.

For instance, let your supplier dream of the day when you'll be their biggest customer. Negotiating a deal on favorable terms will be considerably easier when they perceive your business as a potential long-term client rather than a startup.

One concrete way to accomplish this with a key supplier is to extend the duration of your order rather than just negotiate on price--and, to protect yourself, by adding termination provisions to the contract. Suppliers and their sales staff are more likely to provide a favorable price for a long-term agreement with a termination clause rather than to a small, low volume order. For example, if you're reasonably confident in your business's growth potential, try ordering three years' worth of supplies rather than a one-year supply. But be sure to spread out the payments over the life of the contract and add in an enforceable termination clause.

THE BOTTOM LINE

Sales involves selling your product by gaining support from others so that you can successfully achieve what you have set out to and then assessing your competition and determining price by looking at competitors to make your own product/ service stand out.

Quote from professional:

"You must have a quality product, follow up, be a man of your word, and be in the right market." -Gary Jensen Commercial Construction

Lake Highland | **Entrepreneurs, LLC**

VIII. DISTRIBUTION

Nick Keener
Director of Distribution

- *"In the beginning, my role wasn't very hard, just looking up estimated shipping costs. But once the product comes in, I feel like it's going to get a lot more challenging actually dealing with the process of shipping to our customers."*
- *"Entrepreneurship seems like a very hard skill to master. It takes a lot of perseverance and work to pull off your own business, but if you can do it, the payoff is big."*
- *"My job, as well as the business as a whole just gives me a better look on how businesses are run, as well as the different aspects to each job; mine dealing with distribution."*

"Shoot for the moon, because even if you fail, you will still end up among the stars." -Anonymous

Three Main Points to Distribution:

1. Storing
2. Shipping
3. Profits from Shipping

Storage:

When storing the product, the director of distribution has to oversee the receiving of the product, as well as where it is going to be stored. It has to be stored in a safe place (safe so the product doesn't get damaged) as well as a secure place so the product doesn't get stolen. Also different variables come into storage such as if the product is perishable, it has to be stored in a freezer or refrigerator.

Shipping:

The first part to shipping is making sure the product is documented correctly, with proof of purchase from the customer. It then needs to be packaged correctly, preventing damage. After packaging, it needs to be labeled correctly to make sure its going to the right place and person. The package can be insured if the customer is willing to pay for that service.

Profit:

If the company decides to profit from shipping, it first has to determine the cost it will take to ship the product. Once that is determined, that company can decide on how much they want to profit from shipping. If it costs 5 dollars to ship to a customer, a company may want to charge 7 dollars for shipping in order to gain a 2 dollar profit per unit.

Distribution Director:

This person directs all aspects of the distribution operation including merchandise inventory, shipping and receiving, and maintenance of facilities. Timely deliveries must be ensured to maximize sales. The director must be familiar with a variety of the field's concepts, practices, and procedures and must rely on extensive experience and judgment to plan and accomplish goals. They must also perform a variety of tasks. Leads and directs the work of others. A wide degree of creativity and latitude is expected. Typically reports to top management.

THE BOTTOM LINE

Distribution consists of the storing, packaging, and actual shipping of the product as well as figuring out the price so that the business can profit from it.

Quote from professional:

"Working in corporate America gives you an opportunity to learn and grow while having the guidance and support both psychologically and financially. You have somewhat of a safety net. Being an entrepreneur is very different. No Net!" – Bill Maroon, President of Maroon Fine Homes, Inc.

Alexis Charran
Chief Administration Officer

- *"Administration is as exciting and glamorous as grilled cheese."*
- *"When starting a business, remember there is always someone who can do it better, the real challenge is convincing those people to join your team."*
- *"Entrepreneurialism takes a special kind of person, and this class had made me realize I am one of those people."*

Administration:

* **Hiring an attorney** – when hiring an attorney be sure that you are hiring one that best suits you. Much like doctors and contractors it's okay to shop around. Consider rates and overall chemistry when choosing an attorney. Issues are bound to arise with small business owners and people such as vendors and customers, however it is how they are handled that determines the success of the business. Attorneys can handle anything from the legal startup paper work to yearly taxes. Make sure the payment is fully understood by both parties and don't be afraid to ask for referrals and credentials.

Letter of Engagement:

* **Managing employees** – as officer of administration you will often be asked to keep the employees happy and informed. By filing all the paperwork and keeping the lines of communication open, administration officers ensure that the legalities of the business run smoothly and the task at hand is completed. Most people in the position will be in charge of assisting in managing the demands of both customers and employees, so good people skills are necessary. (http://www.sba.gov/)
* **Advising and setting deadlines** - this ensures the jobs will be designated and completed in a timely manner. Without deadlines it is tough to measure just when sales can begin. A solid knowledge of all fields within the company is ever so useful so that what is asked is within reasonable limits.

Wages:

The Department of Labor enforces the Fair Labor Standards Act (FLSA), which sets basic minimum wage and overtime pay standards. These standards are enforced by the Department's Wage and Hour Division, a program of the Employment Standards Administration.

Workers who are covered by the FLSA are entitled to a minimum wage of not less than $5.85 per hour effective July 24, 2007. Overtime pay at a rate of not less than one and one-half times their regular rate of pay is required after 40 hours of work in a workweek. Certain exemptions apply to specific types of businesses or specific types of work.

In labor and finance settings a *wage* may be defined more narrowly to include only cash paid for some specified quantity (measured in units of time) of labor. Wages may be contrasted with salaries, with wages being paid at a wage rate (based on units of time worked) while salaries are paid periodically without reference to a specified number of hours worked. Once a job description has been established, wages are often a focus when negotiating an employment contract between employer and employee.

Policies:

Creating policies was probably one of the most difficult things encountered at the start of this company. Policies offer a company protection over a wide spectrum with a limited template or foundation.

I, Alexis Charran, and Jaime Leffler came together and started to list what we thought was necessary to operate a business. Because we offered neither wages nor benefits those policies regarding our team were rather simple, making our list very short. It was quite obvious that we needed help and had very little insight into the world of possible disasters in business. It was Mark, of course, who came to our rescue. After some guidance we were able to create policies regarding shipping, return of product, and all payment processes. In the end our policies ensure that both we and the customers are insulated with specific guidelines for any and all transactions.

A policy is a deliberate plan of action to guide decisions and achieve rational outcome(s). The term may apply to government, private sector organizations and groups, and individuals. Presidential executive orders, corporate privacy policies, and parliamentary rules of order are all examples of policy. Policy differs from rules or law. While law can compel or prohibit behaviors (e.g. a law requiring the payment of taxes on income) policy merely guides actions toward those that are most likely to achieve a desired outcome.

Benefits:

When we first started this company all those in the class were expected to maintain the specific role they had been voted into in relation to the company making the ideal of benefits somewhat irrelevant. As a class, 17 members, we are the first in our region to start and run our own business over the course of one semester; which in and of itself is a benefit. Unless you count bragging rights and the satisfaction of a job well done, this company really doesn't compensate us. Due to the time constraints, members don't make more money with time, wages aren't proportional to the amount of effort exerted, and we certainly don't offer medical benefits (and even if we did I doubt any of the students would know what to do with it), thus proving the art of offering benefits isn't one the administration of LHE has mastered.

Pick a job based on how you feel about the work, salary and company future, but know your benefit options, too. There are an infinite number of different benefit packages being offered to college students today, and each of them has its strong and weak points. The key to choosing the best package is to know the options available and the many terms used to describe them.

One important point is that you should never choose a job based solely on the benefit package it offers. This is because benefit programs can change at any time. There are no laws that require companies to maintain any level of benefits, so plans can and do change. Most reputable employers will not suddenly discontinue a benefit, or change it dramatically, but things do happen. Companies change insurance providers, 401K administrators, and that can cause changes in benefits. So – pick jobs based on how you feel about the work, the salary and the future of the company, but know your benefit options (also handy in case you need a tiebreaker).

The first thing to ask is how much of the plan is paid for by the employer and how much of the plan premium do you have to pay. Some employers will now pay 100% of the plan costs (remember – they can change this at any time), but many do not. The next thing to ask is if your premium costs are before or after tax? That means: is your payroll deduction for the premium taken from your Gross (pre-tax) or Net (after-tax) pay. Careful when you ask this - the person answering may not really know. A good question to ask is: "Is this a Section 125 plan?" (Section 125 identifies the portion of the IRS tax code that allows you to pay for insurance with pre-tax dollars.) If you get a blank look, ask that person to find out.

Assume that XYZ Corp pays 50% of a $250 per month premium for good health insurance. LMN.com has the same plan but you have to pay the whole premium. That means that you will pay $1,500 per year more with LMN.com than at XYZ Corp. Simple, right? Now add this wrinkle – XYZ Corp has a plan that lets you pay your share of the premium with pre-tax dollars (the aforementioned Section 125).

And LMN.com makes you pay your cost with after-tax dollars. The difference is not $1,500 ($3,000 vs. $1,500) but $2,500. You have to earn over $4,000 to have the $3,000 Company B wants you to pay - but only $1,500 to pay your premium with Company A.

The only way for major decisions to be made without any havoc is through board meetings where a member must call for a decision and another must second that decision. In order for a board meeting to take place there must always be someone, typically the secretary, who is responsible for taking minutes. Minutes of any meeting are crucial for many reasons – for example if 9 out of the 10 members of the board were present at the company X's board meeting. How would the 10th member know what decisions were made? The most important reason is that minutes are oxygen. If the state claims that the corporation is fake, the easiest and most efficient way out of being shut down is to send the state the companies' minutes. If memberss 1 and 2 have made a major decision outside of a board meeting and didn't mention it at a previous board meeting, the state would have no knowledge regarding the choice. This could end in bad news for the company.

Board Meetings:

Let's say there's a company, X, with ten board members. Board members 1 and 2 decide to make a significant change to the company immediately. The final result would be that the other members would have no clue about the change and lawsuits may be one consequence.

- In a board meeting everything must be seconded by another member. For example if company X was having a meeting then member 6 may say, "I move to open a board meeting" and member 9 would say, "I second that". Member 3, the note taker would record every "move" and every "second" in the minutes.
- In a board meeting, it is essential and common courtesy to follow "Robert's Rules of Order" where in order to speak, a member must be the first to stand once the member who is speaking is finished, but in order to speak a the member must have the Chairman's attention. Board Meetings aren't Kindergarten naptimes – a member who raises his or her hand has no say.
- No debating unless the Chairman calls for a vote

- Any and every motion that is made by board members may be modified, or removed (after being seconded) by other board members before the Chairperson states it.
- No member can speak twice on the same issue unless every member that wants to speak has done so.
- The chairperson is like the judge – all motions must be made to him and in a polite way. NEVER SHOW RUDENESS OR BAD ATTITUDE.
- All time lines (agendas, committee reports, ect.) are merely SUGGESTIONS, which can be voted on for alteration.

THE BOTTOM LINE

Administration is the true behind the scenes work. Without a smoothly run administrative system the company could crumble from the bottom up. Administrators must be responsible and accountable for putting the pieces together allowing the company to be run efficiently and effectively.

Quote from Professional:

"With my abilities of being a hands on type of person and also a very quick learner, I was positive that the business would succeed." -Raymond Charran, Sole Proprietor

X. EXIT STRATEGY

Blake Maher
Director of Mergers and Acquisitions

* *"At first I didn't really know what I was supposed to do and that got me somewhat upset, but now I know about valuing a company and I have learned that it is very important for a business or company. "*
* *"I think entrepreneurship is something everyone should know about whether they are starting their own business or not so they can have that option."*
* *"My job has taught me that there are many aspects in starting, running, and selling your own company. "*
* *"Success means doing the best we can with what we have. Success is the doing, not the getting; in the trying, not the triumph. Success is a personal standard, reaching for the highest that is in us, becoming all that we can be."*

Valuation:

Valuing a company based merely off its assets is the hardest type of business to value. When approaching this type of valuation you must look at everything from customer lists to patents; from books to permits. Everything the company owns comes into play when dealing with valuations. The other two ways to value a company is by sales or by using cash flow or profits. If you are basing it on sales, using a multiplier times the firm's annual sales is the way to go. The multiplier can change as the company changes. It will either boost or drop. Using cash flow or profits is the last way to value a company. To acquire a price you must generate a stream of profit or cash flow. At this point it is all a projection on how much you think the company will make in the next five years or more. Either way, make sure that everything you have is accounted for. Selling a company or business can either be a great hassle or extremely profitable. It all depends on if it is done the right way.

Valuation is the first step toward intelligent investing. When an investor attempts to determine the worth of his or her shares based on the fundamentals, they can make informed decisions about what stocks to buy or sell. Without fundamental value, one is set adrift in a sea of random short-term price movements and gut feelings.

For years, the financial establishment has promoted the specious notion that valuation should be reserved for experts. Supposedly, only sell-side brokerage analysts have the requisite experience and intestinal fortitude to go out into the churning, swirling market and predict future prices. Valuation, however, is no abstruse science that can only be practiced by MBAs and CFAs. Requiring only basic math skills and diligence, any fool can determine values with the best of them.

Before you can value a share of stock, you have to have some notion of what a share of stock is.

A share of stock is not some magical creation that ebbs and flows like the tide; rather, it is the concrete representation of ownership in a publicly traded company. If XYZ Corp. has one million shares of stock outstanding and you hold a single, solitary share, you own a millionth of the company.

Why would someone want to pay you for your millionth? There are quite a few reasons, actually. There is always going to be someone else who wants that millionth of the ownership because they want a millionth of the votes at a shareholder meeting. Although small by itself, if you amass that millionth and about five hundred thousand of its friends, you suddenly have a controlling interest in the company and can make it do all sorts of things, like pay fat dividends or merge with your company.

Companies buy shares in other companies for all sorts of reason. It may be an outright takeover, in which a company buys all the shares, or a joint venture, in which the company typically buys enough of another company to earn a seat on the board of directors, the stock is always on sale. The price of a stock translates into the price of the company, on sale for seven and a half hours a day, five days a week. It is this information that allows other companies, public or private, to make intelligent business decisions with clear and concise information about what another company's shares might cost them.

The share of stock is a stand-in for a share in the company's revenues, earnings, cash flow, shareholder's equity -- you name it, the whole enchilada. For the individual investor, however, this normally means just worrying about what portion of all of those numbers you can get in dividends. The share of ownership entitles you to a share of all dividends in perpetuity. Even if the company's stock does not currently have a dividend yield, there always remains the possibility that at some point in the future there could be some sort of dividend.

Finally, a company can simply repurchase its own shares using its excess cash, rather than paying out dividends to shareholders. This effectively drives up the stock price by providing a buyer as well as improving earnings per share (EPS) comparisons by decreasing the number of shares outstanding. Mature, cash-flow positive companies tend to be much more liberal in this day and age with share repurchases as opposed to dividends, simply because dividends to shareholders get taxed twice.

This series of articles will take you through the major methods for valuing companies. The main categories of valuation I will elucidate are valuations based on earnings, revenues, cash flow, equity, dividends and subscribers. Finally, I will sum this all up in a conclusion that positions these valuations in the broader context of fundamental analysis and gives you a sense of how to apply these in your own investment efforts.

Selling your business:

If your business has been a success, you've probably had to pour most of your time, energy, and money into it for what may seem like forever. You may see your company as an extension of yourself, and it may be hard to even imagine life without it. In some cases your entire family may have depended on the business, discussed it endlessly around the dinner table, used it as an education and a proving ground for the children, and practically made it into another family member!

On the other hand, your business may have been only marginally successful, and something you can't wait to get rid of. Or, perhaps you entered into the business with the idea that it would be a short-term opportunity and that you'd sell out whenever you got a decent offer.

Whatever your situation, selling your business will be one of the most important things you'll ever do, because unlike virtually every other business decision you've made over the years, *you'll only do this once*. You get a single chance to put a price tag on possibly years and years of effort — and once you sign the sales documents, it's over.

You'll come out way ahead, both financially and personally, if you make an effort to understand the steps in selling, formulate your plan carefully with the help of your professional advisors, and, when the time comes, take the time to negotiate a price and terms that satisfy your reasons for getting out of the business.

Even if you think you're many years away from selling out, you should consider what your heirs or successors would have to do if you died unexpectedly. If you don't have a workable exit strategy in place, you (or your heirs) may have no choice but to liquidate the business and sell off the assets piecemeal; getting *nothing* for the goodwill you've built up over the course of the years.

Here are the major issues you need to think about when it's time to sell your business:

- Initial issues in selling out: how should you time your decision and choose experts to help, and what legal/ethical pitfalls do you need to avoid?

- Valuations of small businesses: how does the market put a price on a small business, and what can you do to maximize your own business's value?

- Finding a buyer: what do you need to know about working with a business broker, creating a selling memorandum, and other marketing concerns?

- Structuring the deal: what are your options as to terms, paying particular attention to the tax implications of various alternatives?

- Financing the deal: what should you know about seller financing, and third-party financing through leveraged buyouts?

- Completing the deal: from the Letter of Intent through due diligence to the closing, what are the typical steps you can expect to go through in the sales process?

THE BOTTOM LINE

Determining the value of your product/service is imperative to the future of your company telling you whether it is a smart idea to continue progress or sell it when it is at its peak of profit to you, the creator. It is all about weighing your losses and seeing into the future… however impossible that may seem.

Quote from professional:

"The keys to profitability; you, your crew, and office staff. They can make or break you." –Mark Ramsay, President of Golf Range Netting

XI. LAKE HIGHLAND ENTREPRENEURS

What We've Learned

I.		Macro economic concepts
	1.	Contracts, corporations, and accountability
II.		The Cost of Living
III.		Various ways to create wealth
IV.		Banking
	1.	Loans, interest and business checking
V.		Accounting
	1.	P&L Statement, Pro forma Statement, & EBITDA
VI.		Hiring a Lawyer
	1.	Signing Contracts
VII.		Running the Business
	1.	Writing a Business Plan
	2.	Brainstorming Techniques
	3.	Robert's Rules of Order
	4.	Electing/Hiring Executives
VIII.		Hiring a Public Relations Firm
IX.		Starting an Effective Marketing Campaign
X.		Getting Investors
XI.		Producing a Product
XII.		Selling a Product

Experience

Walking into this company with very little experience,17 high school students accomplished the unexpected; starting and running their own company.

XII. SPONSORS

SPECIAL THANKS:

> Warren Hudson
> Bob VanDer Lugt
> Kathy Taylor
> Jane Buecher
> Chirag Kabrawala
> Mark Hayes
> Jason Schmidt
> Jim Zboril
> Steve Cady
> Steven Steward

SPONSORS:

> Atlantic Management, Inc.
> Consensus Communications
> Latham, Shuker, Eden and Bodein
> Lake Highland Preparatory School
> Bank First
> Nitesol, Inc.

INVESTORS:

> Johnnie P. James
> John Hurlburt
> Michael Grindstaff
> Christine Maddux
> Jane Buecher
> Ralph Martinez

XIII. APPENDIX

References:

AAMC. *New AAMC Study Finds Medical Schools and Teaching Hospitals are Major Economic Contributors.* February 4, 2005.

Business Facilities. "2005 Rankings Report, Top States for Biotech Growth," December 1, 2005.

Craver, Richard. "Study puts priority on research-park projects," *Winston-Salem Journal.* December 1, 2005.

Ellis, Rafaela. "A living, a diverse population makes Central Florida the perfect Petri dish for medical research," Texture. June 2005.

Enterprise Florida. *Comprehensive Life Sciences Study to Jumpstart Florida Cluster Development Strategy.* June 8, 2005.

Enterprise Florida. *Roadmap to Florida's Future, 2005 Annual Report.* 2005.

Enterprise Florida. *The Florida Economy at a Glance.* September 2005.

Enterprise Florida. *The Impact of Scripps Florida on Florida's Economy.* November 2004.

Enterprise Florida. *Diversifying Florida's Economy: Priority Recommendations.*

Florida Board of Governors. *Y-Axis Report of BOG Strategic Plan.*

Florida International University. *Board of Governor's Presentation.*

Florida.high.tech. The *Guide to Florida's High Tech Corridor.* 2005.

Florida Tax Watch. *Funding New Biomedical Research Center is an Ideal Use of Florida's Federal Economic Development Funds.* October 17, 2005.

Hickey, Terry. *UCF Response to the Division of Colleges and Universities on the MGT Study of Cost-per-degree and Targeted Programs.* February 1, 2005.

MGT of America, Inc. *Analysis of Degree Production Goals and Institutional Plans for Board of Governors Strategic Planning Workshop.* February 9, 2005.

Milken Institute. *America's Biotech and Life Science Clusters.* June 2004.

Milken Institute. *The Greater Philadelphia Life Sciences Cluster: An Economic and Comparative Assessment.* June 2005.

Milken Institute. *Best Performing Cities: Where America's Jobs are Created and Sustained.* November 2004.

State University System of Florida. *Florida Board of Governors Strategic Plan 2005-2013.* June 9, 2005.

The Florida Council of 100. *We Must Do Better! Moving Florida's State University System to the Next Level in Quality and Accessibility.* January 2004.

The Washington Economics Group, Inc. *The Economic Impact of Scripps Florida Biotech Research Institute.* October 9, 2003.

The Washington Economics Group, Inc. *Brief- The Economic Impact Of The Proposed University Of Central Florida College Of Medicine.* November 9, 2005.

The Washington Economics Group, Inc. *An Assessment of Factors Affecting the Progress Toward Achieving the Projected Biotech Industry Cluster Associated with TSRI's Operation in Florida: First Year Analysis.* November 29, 2004

University of Central Florida Medical School Task Force. *Medical School Initiative in Central Florida.* 2005.

University of Central Florida. *Request to Establish a New Medical School to the Florida Board of Governors.*

The Free Dictionary. [Online] 17 March 2008. <http://www.thefreedictionary.com/entrepreneurialism>.

Info Mean Blog. [Online] 17 March 2008. < http://blog.infomean.com/the-new-paradigm-for-entrepreneurial-success/>.

The Free Encyclopedia, Wikipedia. [Online] 18 March 2008. <http://en.wikipedia.org/wiki/Administration_%28business%290>.

"Effective Leadership". [Online] 20 March 2008. <http://www.1000ventures.com/business_guide/crosscuttings/leadership_main.html>.

"What is Trust?" [Online] 20 March 2008. <http://changingminds.org/explanations/trust/what_is_trust.htm>.

Mallinson, Wayne. "The Importance of Attitude." [Online] 21 March 2008. <http://www.sacareerfocus.co.za/content_sub.cfm?AgentsID=302&PageID=498&SubPageID=544>.

Rodriguez, George. "How to Develop a Winning Sales Plan." [Online] 25 March 2008. <http://www.powerhomebiz.com/062006/salesplan.htm>.

Haumann, Roger. "Getting Your Name Out There." [Online] 25 March 2008. <http://www.netclick.com.au/articles/9799/1/Getting-Your-Name-Out-There/Page1.html>.

"How to Create a Product Presentation." [Online] 25 March 2008. <http://www.infrasystems.com/product-presentations.html>.

"7 Steps to Investing." [Online] 26 March 2008. <http://investsmartvt.castleton.edu/pdfs/7%20steps%20to%20investing.pdf>.

"Understanding Your Target Market." [Online] 24 March 2008. <http://www.allbusiness.com/marketing/segmentation-targeting/848-1.html>.
"Determining the Target Audience of Your Small Business." [Online] 26 March 2008. <http://www.allbusiness.com/marketing/segmentation-targeting/2588-1.html>.

American Research Group Inc. "Ten Rules For More Effective Advertising." [Online] 29 March 2008. <http://americanresearchgroup.com/adrules/>.

Bellis, Mary. "Marketing Plan for the Independent Inventor." [Online] 30 March 2008. <http://inventors.about.com/od/advertisingmedia/a/effective_marke.htm>.

Williams, John. "Target the Right Niche." [Online] 30 March 2008. <http://www.entrepreneur.com/marketing/branding/imageandbrandingcolumnistjohnwilliams/article178964.html>.

"Marketing Your Product." [Online] 30 March 2008. <http://www.toolkit.com/small_business_guide/sbg.aspx?nid=P03_0101>.

"How to Get People Talking About Your Product." [Online] 30 March 2008. <http://www.ericsink.com/articles/Buzz.html>.

The Free Encyclopedia, Wikipedia. "Product Marketing." [Online] 30 March 2008. <http://en.wikipedia.org/wiki/Product_marketing>.

Advani, Asheesh. "Negotiation Tips for Startups." [Online] 1 April 2008. <http://www.entrepreneur.com/money/financing/startupfinancingcolumnistasheeshadvani/article76894.html>.

U.S Department of Labor. "Wages" [Online] 1 April 2008. <http://www.dol.gov/dol/topic/wages/>.

The Free Encyclopedia, Wikipedia. "Wage." [Online] 1 April 2008. <http://en.wikipedia.org/wiki/Wage>.

The Free Encyclopedia, Wikipedia. "Policy." [Online] 3 April 2008. <http://en.wikipedia.org/wiki/Public_policy>.

"Introduction to Valuation." [Online] 3 April 2008. <http://www.fool.com/School/IntroductionToValuation.htm>.

"Selling Your Business." [Online] 4 April 2008. <http://www.toolkit. com/small_business_guide/sbg.aspx?nid=P11_2000>.

Investopedia. "Debt/Equity." [Online] 10 April 2008.

<http://www.investopedia.com/terms/d/debtequityratio. asp>.

Volker, Mike. "Profit & Loss Projections." [Online] 10 April 2008. <http://www.sfu.ca/~mvolker/biz/pl.htm>.

"Creating a Profit and Loss Statement." [Online] 10 April 2008. <http://www.va-interactive.com/inbusiness/editorial/ finance/intemp/income.html>.

"Financial Planning." [Online] 10 April 2008. <http://financialplan.about.com/library/howto/htbudget. htm>.

Kenny, Joseph. "Things to Look for in an Investment." [Online] 10 April 2008. <http://knowhow-now.com/Finance-article65347- ThingsToLookForInAnInvestment.html>.

Money Instructor. "What is Accounting?" [Online] 11 April 2008. <http://www.moneyinstructor.com/lesson/accountingintro. asp>.

Roberts Rules. "Roberts Rules of Order." [Online] 20 April 2008. <http://www.rulesonline.com>